Feminicity

THE BELLY DANCE AWAKENING

Joany Gauvreau

BALBOA.PRESS
A DIVISION OF HAY HOUSE

Copyright © 2024 Joany Gauvreau.

All rights reserved. No part of this book may be used or reproduced by any means, graphic, electronic, or mechanical, including photocopying, recording, taping or by any information storage retrieval system without the written permission of the author except in the case of brief quotations embodied in critical articles and reviews.

Balboa Press books may be ordered through booksellers or by contacting:

Balboa Press
A Division of Hay House
1663 Liberty Drive
Bloomington, IN 47403
www.balboapress.com
844-682-1282

Because of the dynamic nature of the Internet, any web addresses or links contained in this book may have changed since publication and may no longer be valid. The views expressed in this work are solely those of the author and do not necessarily reflect the views of the publisher, and the publisher hereby disclaims any responsibility for them.

The author of this book does not dispense medical advice or prescribe the use of any technique as a form of treatment for physical, emotional, or medical problems without the advice of a physician, either directly or indirectly. The intent of the author is only to offer information of a general nature to help you in your quest for emotional and spiritual well-being. In the event you use any of the information in this book for yourself, which is your constitutional right, the author and the publisher assume no responsibility for your actions.

Any people depicted in stock imagery provided by Getty Images are models, and such images are being used for illustrative purposes only.
Certain stock imagery © Getty Images.

Print information available on the last page.

ISBN: 979-8-7652-5789-0 (sc)
ISBN: 979-8-7652-5790-6 (e)

Library of Congress Control Number: 2024925183

Balboa Press rev. date: 12/18/2024

CONTENTS

Preface ix

Welcome xv

Chapter 1: Beyond the Veil of Movement 1
- Unveil the Power of Ancient Rhythms   4
- Belly Dance's Historical and Cultural Significance   5
- Belly Dance: Beyond Physical Fitness   8
- Holistic Integration Through Belly Dance   9
- Personal Growth Opportunities Within Belly Dance   10

Chapter 2: The Dance of Energies 13
- The Rise of Femininity: Connecting with the Divine Feminine Within   16
- Balancing Feminine and Masculine Energies: The Path to Wholeness   17
- Activating the Chakras: A Journey Through the Body's Energy Centers   19
- The CHAKRA Model: Cultivating Harmony Through Activating Key Rhythmic Alignments   20
- Exploring Each Chakra   22
- Implementing the CHAKRA Model   25

Chapter 3: Anatomic Harmony: The Body's Symphony 27
- Discovering Anatomic Harmony Through the Symphony of Belly Dance   29
    - The Core: Igniting the Fire Within   29

- o   The Spine: A Pillar of Strength and Flexibility — 29
- o   The Pelvis: A Cradle of Creation and Expression — 30
- o   The Fascia: Weaving a Web of Connectivity — 30
- Unlock the Symphony Within: Harmonizing Body and Spirit Through Dance — 31
- Activating the Senses for Emotional and Spiritual Well-Being — 31

Chapter 4: Rhythms of the Soul 32

- Unleash the Symphony Within: Harnessing Music for Wholeness — 36
- The Rhythmic Synergy of Movement and Music — 36
- Embrace Your Inner Rhythm: A Journey into the Richness of Arabic Music — 37
- Music as Your Dance Partner — 38
- Mindfulness in Belly Dance — 38
- Practical Steps to Harness Music for Wholeness — 39
- Creating Your Dance Playlist — 40
- Resources for Deepening Your Musical Journey — 40
- Integrating Music into Your Daily Life — 41
- Conclusion: Your Unique Musical Journey — 42

Chapter 5: Unveiling the Dance Within 43

- Shedding the Shadows: Embracing the Light of Belly Dance — 46
- Steps to Embracing Your Dance Journey — 47
- Unraveling the Misconceptions and Fears Surrounding Belly Dance — 48
- Cultivating Empowerment Through Self-Expression — 49

Chapter 6: The Inner Dance of Discovery 52

- Unlocking the Essence of Transformation Through Ancient Rhythms — 55
- Cultivating Body Awareness, Vulnerability, and Self-Compassion — 56

- The Importance of Regular Practice and Cultural Immersion — 57
- Approaching Belly Dance with an Open Heart — 58
- The Alchemy of Movement and Music — 59
- Embrace the Journey — 60

Chapter 7: Embodying the Elements 61
- Dancing with the Rhythms of Nature: Elemental Alchemy in Belly Dance — 64
  - The Earth Element: Grounding and Stability — 64
  - The Water Element: Fluidity and Grace — 65
  - The Fire Element: Passion and Intensity — 66
  - The Air Element: Freedom and Expansion — 67
- The Harmonious Dance of the Elements — 68
- Incorporating Elemental Awareness in Daily Life — 69

Chapter 8: Reclaiming Your Life's Rhythm 70
- Unleash Your True Potential: The Transformative Power of Belly Dance — 73
- Understanding Belly Dance's Role in Emotional Healing and Spiritual Awakening — 74
- Emotional and Spiritual Dimensions of Movement — 75
- Integrating Belly Dance into Holistic Recovery — 75
- Embracing Belly Dance for Holistic Well-Being and a Transformative Journey — 76

Chapter 9: The Unexpected Call to Connect 80
- Culminating Insights: Deepening Power and Connection Through Belly Dance — 85
- Embracing the Holistic Impact of Belly Dance — 85
- Integrating Belly Dance into Life for Balance and Fulfillment — 86
- Leveraging Belly Dance for Community Connection and Personal Growth — 86

- Conclusion: A Continuing Journey of Joy and Self-Discovery Through Belly Dance　　87

Epilogue **89**
- The Journey Continues　　89

Addendum: Guide to Movements and Music for Elemental Energies, Feminine/Masculine Balance, and Chakra Activation **93**
- Feminine/Masculine Energy Balance　　94
- Chakra Activation　　96
- Future Exploration: Twelve Chakra Belly Dance　　99
- Elemental Energies　　100
- Resources　　104

PREFACE

> Dance is the movement of the universe
> concentrated in an individual.
> —Isadora Duncan

Imagine a dance form so powerful that it harmonizes your life's rhythms with ancient wisdom while naturally enhancing your physical vitality and well-being. Belly dance, with its mesmerizing undulations, rhythmic hip movements, and expressive gestures, is not just an art—it's a holistic journey that unites body, mind, and spirit.

My journey with belly dance began in the small town of Sturgeon Falls, Northern Ontario, Canada. As a child, I was a sports enthusiast, more likely to be found skating or playing ringette at the ice arena or on the volleyball court than in a dance studio. In our hockey town, belly dance was practically nonexistent. No one belly danced, and like me, no one even knew of its existence.

Before discovering belly dance, I led a sedentary life, working for Statistics Canada as a business profiler. At my heaviest, I weighed 215 pounds. My transformation began when I stumbled upon a book titled *The Art of Belly Dance: A Fun and Fabulous Way to Get Fit* by Carolena Nericcio. What initially caught my attention was the promise of getting fit while having fun. At that point, I truly had no idea what belly dance was.

Intrigued by the concept, I followed the instructions in the book, gradually incorporating more books and other resources like DVDs into my self-taught practice. For a year, I dedicated myself to learning and practicing belly dance on my own. The results were transformative—not only had I discovered a new passion but I also lost seventy pounds in the process.

As a thirty-four-year-old single mother grappling with depression and an eating disorder, I discovered belly dancing through that book, and it sparked my curiosity. This simple activity soon evolved into an essential therapeutic tool, significantly enhancing my physical health and revitalizing my emotional and spiritual well-being. Each step, each undulation, and each shimmy allowed me to connect with my body, my emotions, and my spirit in a way that I had never experienced before.

Unlike many dancers, I didn't follow the usual path of training and performing before becoming a teacher. Instead, I was called to teaching right from the start. My background in aerobics naturally blended with belly dance, creating a unique fusion that resonated with many, offering both the joy of dance and the gentle cultivation of strength and flexibility. As my classes grew in popularity, I recognized an opportunity to expand our dance experience through performance. Despite my lack of stage experience, I felt compelled to showcase the grace, strength, and artistic beauty of belly dance.

As I delved deeper into the practice, guided by the wisdom found within the pages of that introductory book, I realized that belly dance was more than just a form of self-expression; it was a powerful catalyst for personal transformation. It wasn't until I began exploring holistic healing techniques and other somatic modalities that I could put words to the incredible sensations and experiences I had while dancing. I soon realized that the dance was activating and balancing my chakras, the body's energy centers, leading me to a greater sense of wholeness and well-being. Incorporating holistic, somatic, and esoteric modalities into my belly dance practice enhances my physical agility, emotional well-being, and spiritual connectedness, allowing me to dance with greater fluidity, purpose, and harmony.

This realization further fueled my passion for belly dance and its transformative power. As I continued on this path of self-discovery, I found that belly dance not only helped me heal from my personal wounds but also gave me the tools to help others on their journeys of transformation. This inspired me to open my own dance studio and to later develop "Feminicity," dedicated to exploring the transformative benefits of dance.

Belly dance serves as an expansive umbrella, sheltering a rich diversity of sacred dances that trace their roots back to ancient times and distant lands. This ancient lineage infuses the dance with a profound sense of connection—to the past, to the divine feminine, and to the elemental forces of nature. When we engage in belly dance, we participate in a living, breathing tradition passed down through generations of women.

Through this work, I've witnessed countless individuals walk through my studio doors seeking one thing but finding so much more—a deeper connection to themselves and a vibrant, supportive community. These stories of personal transformation and growth have been a constant source of inspiration, fueling my desire to share the sacred belly dance with a wider audience.

Belly dance has also helped me develop the practice of gratitude, which has become an essential part of my healing and growth journey. By consciously acknowledging the gifts, lessons, and transformative experiences I've encountered along the way, I've learned to shift my focus from challenges and setbacks to blessings and opportunities for growth. Expressing gratitude for the dance itself, for the wisdom of my mind and body, and for the supportive individuals who have guided and inspired me has become a daily ritual that has profoundly enhanced my personal evolution.

As I found love for myself through dance, I attracted loving relationships into my life. I've been married not once but twice—first at forty-two and again at fifty years young. Both times, I found partners who loved me unconditionally. This deep, unconditional love is something I was only able to receive because I had allowed it to flourish within me, nurtured by the self-respect and authenticity I discovered through belly dancing.

I have come to understand that gratitude is not merely a response to positive experiences but a powerful catalyst for creating more joy, abundance, and healing in my life. My mission with this book is to extend this transformative experience to you, helping you to find joy, healing, and balance in your life without succumbing to society's limits. This book is crafted for seekers—those who are curious and open-minded, yearning for a melding of the physical with the metaphysical. No prior dance experience is necessary, only a desire to engage with your body in new ways and explore the depths of your emotions.

Through vivid descriptions and sensory-rich guidance, I invite you into the world of belly dance where each movement is an expression of life itself, where music is a critical partner enhancing every emotional and energetic shift. By engaging with this book, you're investing in a journey of self-discovery. You can expect to encounter a blend of structured choreography and spontaneous improvisation that mirrors life's rhythms. Anticipate feeling empowered as you balance your feminine and masculine energies, tapping into an ancient wisdom that views the body as a map of spiritual growth.

As we embark on this journey together, remember that belly dancing isn't just about learning movements; it's about raising your vibrational frequency from lower emotional states to the higher vibrations of joy and love. It's about transforming not just your body but your entire being.

As you delve deeper into *Feminicity: The Belly Dance Awakening*, remember that this book is more than just a guide to learning belly dance; it is the answer to the question of "why belly dance?" The stories shared within these pages are based on true events, though names have been changed to protect privacy. These are stories that we can all relate to in some way, detailing personal journeys of healing, self-discovery, empowerment, and the reclamation of sovereignty; stories that resonate with our own experiences and aspirations. Through these narratives, you'll discover how belly dance can be a powerful tool for asserting your autonomy, setting healthy boundaries, and standing firmly in your own power.

This book explores the transformative power of belly dance. It is a resource for those seeking to harmonize their lives through ancient rhythms and to connect deeply with themselves on a physical, emotional, and spiritual level. Through this exploration, you'll not only experience the movements of belly dance but also its profound ability to awaken your inner wisdom, elevate your vibrational frequency, and guide you toward a more joyful, balanced, and authentic life.

Thank you for allowing me into your world through these pages. I am excited for you to continue reading, exploring, and discovering the rich tapestries of health, happiness, and harmony that await.

Welcome, beautiful soul,

In the shimmies and undulations of belly dance, we awaken the sacred feminine within ourselves. Each movement is more than just steps—it's a reclaiming of our power, a celebration of life, and a joyful expression of our authentic selves. Every breath we take is a reminder of the divine essence that lives within us.

As you turn these pages, I invite you to embrace this transformative journey with open arms and an open heart. May you discover the dancer who has always been waiting to emerge, radiant in her power, grace, and beauty.

Welcome to the healing world of belly dance. Welcome home to yourself.

Let's dance our way to healing, empowerment, and joy together. The journey begins now—are you ready?

—Joany

1

BEYOND THE VEIL OF MOVEMENT

Sylvia stood nervously at the entrance of the community center, her heart pounding with a mixture of excitement and apprehension. The faint strains of Middle Eastern music drifted through the air, beckoning her toward the dance studio where her first-ever belly dance class was about to start. At thirty-five, Sylvia had always been curious about this ancient art form but had never found the courage to try it until now.

As she hesitated at the threshold, Sylvia reflected on what had brought her here. The past year had been challenging—a stressful job, the end of a long-term relationship, and a general feeling of being disconnected from her body and her authentic self. She had stumbled upon a video of a belly dance performance online, and something about the fluid movements and joyful expression of the dancer had sparked a longing within her. The dancer seemed to embody a sense of strength and grace that Sylvia yearned to develop in herself.

Taking a deep breath, Sylvia stepped into the studio. The room was filled with women of all ages and body types, some looking as nervous as she was, others chatting excitedly. The walls were adorned with colorful tapestries and images depicting the rich history of belly dance.

The instructor, a graceful woman wearing vibrant, jingling coin-embellished attire, approached Sylvia with an air of warmth and encouragement. Her eyes sparkled with a mixture of wisdom and excitement as she welcomed her to the ancient art of belly dance.

As the class began, Sylvia felt both excitement and self-consciousness. The instructor started by sharing a brief history of belly dance, explaining its roots in Middle Eastern and North African cultures, and its significance as both a social dance and a form of cultural expression. This context helped Sylvia feel like she was participating in something much larger than a simple fitness class.

Each movement, from the basic hip circles to the fluid arm patterns, felt both foreign and strangely familiar to Sylvia. It was as if her body had been waiting for this moment, ready to speak a language it had always known but had never been allowed to use. The instructor explained how these movements were not just choreography but expressions of elemental energies—the grounding of earth, the flow of water, the passion of fire, and the freedom of air.

Throughout the class, Sylvia alternated between moments of pure joy as she lost herself in the music and movements, and pangs of self-doubt as she struggled with physical coordination. She found herself comparing her awkward attempts to the graceful movements of more experienced dancers. However, the instructor's gentle reminders to focus on the feeling of the movements rather than their appearance helped Sylvia relax and enjoy the experience.

As the class progressed, Sylvia began to notice subtle changes. The instructor guided them through movements said to activate different energy centers in the body, or chakras. She was surprised to find that certain movements seemed to release tension she didn't even know she was holding. She started to focus on the connection between her breath and her movements, finding a rhythm that felt natural and soothing.

By the end of the class, Sylvia was surprised to find herself smiling, her body humming with newfound energy. The instructor approached her, noticing Sylvia's mix of excitement and contemplation. "How did you find your first experience with this ancient art?" she asked warmly.

Sylvia hesitated, then let her thoughts flow. "It was … fascinating. I felt like I was connecting to something so much older and deeper than just a dance class. There were moments when I felt awkward but also times when I felt surprisingly ... whole."

The teacher nodded, her eyes lighting up. "That's the beauty of belly dance. It's an art form that dates back thousands of years, with roots in Middle Eastern and North African cultures. What you're feeling is the dance's ability to integrate mind, body, and spirit. It's not just about the movements but also about tapping into a tradition that has long been used for celebration, healing, and self-expression. Some believe it even helps balance our energy centers, or chakras. As you continue, you may find it offers benefits far beyond physical exercise—an emotional release, stress reduction, increased body awareness, and a profound sense of being connected to yourself and others."

As Sylvia left the studio that day, she felt a spark of excitement ignite within. She couldn't wait to return for the next class, to lose herself in the dance once more, and to delve deeper into this ancient practice. For the first time in what felt like forever, she looked forward to exploring this form of self-expression and the holistic journey of self-discovery it promised.

Little did Sylvia know that her journey into the world of belly dance was about to open doors she never knew existed, leading her on a path of physical, emotional, and spiritual transformation that would change her life in ways she could never have imagined. The ancient rhythms had begun to awaken something deep within, calling her to explore the rich tapestry of this timeless art form and the profound wisdom it held.

> To dance is to be out of yourself. Larger,
> more beautiful, more powerful. It is glory
> on Earth and it is yours for the taking.
> —Agnes De Mille

Joany Gauvreau

UNVEIL THE POWER OF ANCIENT RHYTHMS

As we delve deeper into the world of belly dance, it becomes clear that this ancient art form is not merely a physical practice but also a powerful form of energy medicine. Each fluid movement, each graceful gesture, has the potential to activate and harmonize the body's intricate energy systems, promoting healing and balance on every level.

When we engage in belly dance, we stimulate the flow of vital energy along the meridians, those invisible pathways that carry our life force throughout our bodies. We awaken the chakras, the spinning vortexes of light that govern our physical, emotional, and spiritual well-being. We also activate the radiant circuits, the extraordinary vessels that connect us to the universal field of energy that surrounds and sustains us.

Studies over the past two decades have shed light on the physiological benefits of belly dance. An early influential study by Abrão and Pedrão (2005) published in the *Journal of Physical Activity and Health* found that belly dancing significantly improves body composition, flexibility, and muscular endurance in adult women.

More recent research has continued to support and expand on those findings. For instance, a study by Na Nongkhai et al. (2014) published in the *Journal of Science and Technology* demonstrated the positive effects of belly dancing on obese women when combined with nutritional education. This study, conducted as part of the Obesity Clinic Projects at Community Health Center, showed significant improvements in body mass index (BMI), body fat percentage, and lipid profiles among participants.

Through the undulating waves of a snake arm or the grounded power of an earthy hip drop, we can target specific energy pathways, releasing blockages and restoring harmony to our being. In the shimmering vibrations of a belly roll or the soaring freedom of a veil dance, we can tap into the boundless potential of our own life force, igniting the spark of transformation within.

Belly dance, often perceived merely as an enchanting form of entertainment or physical exercise, holds much deeper significance. This dance form is a gateway to personal transformation and holistic well-being. Through rhythmic movements synchronized with breath and music, dancers tap into deeper layers of their psyche, releasing stored emotions while fostering a rejuvenated sense of self. Each movement is not only physical but also an emotional expression and spiritual experience, allowing individuals to manage stress and connect with a higher purpose. The intricate motions help balance energy centers, or chakras, facilitating the smooth flow of energy throughout the body.

A 2020 study in the *International Journal of Environmental Research and Public Health* found that belly dancing had positive effects on body image and self-esteem in women, supporting its potential for psychological well-being (Tiggemann et al. 2020).

As dancers become attuned to their bodies, they gain confidence and strength, which extend beyond the dance floor, enabling them to handle challenges with grace and resilience. This chapter lays foundational concepts that resonate throughout the book—focusing on the alchemy of movement with music, creating an emotional release; choreography paired with improvisation, mirroring life; balancing feminine and masculine energies; connecting with natural elements; activating chakras for balance; and raising vibrational frequencies to elevate an overall sense of well-being.

By integrating these elements into your practice through exercises in each section, you will enhance your physical fitness and embark on a journey toward emotional healing and spiritual discovery. This holistic approach ensures that every step in belly dancing brings you closer to achieving a harmonious life balance.

Thus, as we delve into the depths of belly dance, remember that each sway and spiral is not just a movement—it's energy; it's transformation; it's an awakening.

BELLY DANCE'S HISTORICAL AND CULTURAL SIGNIFICANCE

The origins of belly dance weave an intricate tapestry, stretching back to the dawn of civilization. Its sinuous movements and rhythmic undulations echo through millennia from the ancient lands of

Mesopotamia, Egypt, and surrounding regions. This impressive lineage infuses the dance with a timeless connection to the past, embodying the divine feminine and the elemental forces of nature.

Engravings in pharaonic temples offer tangible evidence of belly dance's ancient roots, depicting figures performing movements strikingly similar to modern iterations. These archaeological finds indicate that the dance played an integral role in religious and cultural ceremonies of antiquity. Scholars posit that these ancient dances were intimately linked to fertility rites and the worship of goddesses, serving as a celebration of the divine feminine and the cyclical nature of life.

Anthropological studies have further illuminated belly dance's historical significance. Many researchers theorize that the dance originated as a fertility ritual, specifically designed to prepare women for childbirth and to honor the female body's strength and resilience. As civilizations rose and fell across the ages, belly dance evolved in tandem, absorbing and reflecting diverse cultural influences while steadfastly maintaining its core essence.

Contrary to popular misconceptions, belly dance was not primarily a form of entertainment for men. Instead, it flourished as a women's art form, practiced in private spaces where women gathered to celebrate milestones, strengthen community bonds, and pass their wisdom down through generations. This tradition of female empowerment and camaraderie remains a cornerstone of belly dance culture today.

The spiritual dimensions of belly dance align with other movement-based practices that seek transcendence through physical expression. The Sufi practice of whirling, for example, shares common ground with belly dance in its use of rhythmic movement to achieve altered states of consciousness. Both practices demonstrate the universal power of dance as a means of connecting with the divine and exploring the depths of human experience.

Today, belly dance encompasses a rich tapestry of styles, each with its own unique characteristics and cultural influences. While the diversity of belly dance is vast and ever evolving, here are just a few examples that showcase its breadth.

Egyptian Raqs sharqi: This style is more grounded and intricate, with smaller, more controlled movements. It emphasizes fluidity and grace, with a focus on detailed hip movements and expressive arm gestures.

Turkish Oryantal Dans: These movements are typically energetic and dynamic, featuring numerous spins, high kicks, and displays of athleticism. There is a strong emphasis on dramatic arm and body movements.

American Tribal Style (ATS): This is a modern fusion dance style that emphasizes improvisation within a group. Dancers use a system of cues to lead and follow, creating synchronized performances. The movements are strong and grounded, drawing from various global dance traditions.

Sacred Dance: This form of dance infuses movements with spiritual significance and is often used in rituals or meditative practices. The movements are intentional and carry deep spiritual meaning.

Tribal Fusion: This is an evolution of American Tribal Style, blending traditional belly dance techniques with contemporary aesthetics and elements from other dance forms like hip-hop and modern dance. It allows for a high degree of personal expression and creativity.

These styles represent only a fraction of the myriad forms that belly dance has taken across cultures and throughout history. From the traditional to the avant-garde, from solo performances to group improvisations, the world of belly dance continues to grow and adapt, reflecting the creativity and diversity of its practitioners.

By engaging with any of these styles, practitioners become part of a vibrant, global community. This worldwide network of dancers is united not just by a shared passion but also by a living tradition that continues to evolve while honoring its ancient roots.

As we embrace the full breadth and depth of belly dance, we open ourselves to a richer experience of this transformative art. It offers a path to self-discovery, cultural appreciation, and personal growth. Whether performed in a sacred temple, at a family gathering, or on a modern stage, belly dance continues to speak to the human spirit, celebrating the beauty and power of the body in motion.

BELLY DANCE: BEYOND PHYSICAL FITNESS

Belly dance is fundamentally a transformative journey that transcends mere physical exercise. It's a holistic practice that nurtures not only the body but also the mind and spirit. Unlike conventional workouts that primarily focus on physical endurance and muscle strength, belly dance engages the dancer in a profound rhythmic experience that harmonizes internal energies.

A study in the *International Journal of Sport and Exercise Psychology* found that belly dance practitioners reported higher levels of body appreciation and embodiment compared to nondancers, suggesting its potential for improving body image and self-concept (Swami & Tovée, 2014).

The movement in belly dance is like the flow of a river—continuous and soothing yet powerful in its ability to reshape the landscape.

Just as a river carves its path through the land with grace and strength, belly dance movements sculpt the dancer's body and soul, moving beyond physical fitness into realms of emotional expression and spiritual awakening.

Each sway and hip drop in belly dance serves more than an aesthetic function; they are gateways to a deeper self-awareness. As dancers move to the rhythms, they connect with their inner selves, often uncovering emotions and energies that have long been suppressed or unacknowledged. This emotional release is not just therapeutic; it's also transformative, fostering a greater sense of personal well-being and emotional health.

Furthermore, belly dancing also promotes mindfulness and presence. The concentration required to execute the intricate movements helps clear the mind of daily stresses and cultivates a focused calmness similar to that achieved through meditation. This mindful practice encourages a state of mental clarity in which one can find sanctuary from the chaos of everyday life.

At its core, belly dance is not just about achieving physical fitness but about embarking on a transformative journey that integrates body, heart, and spirit.

HOLISTIC INTEGRATION THROUGH BELLY DANCE

> **Dance is the ultimate expression of exuberance that your body can find.**
> **—Sadhguru**

In belly dance, every movement is an interplay of the physical form with its emotional currents and spiritual energies. This integration manifests a holistic form of well-being that is seldom achieved through other forms of exercise. When you step into the world of belly dance, you not only engage your muscles but also tap into your emotional vulnerabilities and spiritual yearnings.

The holistic nature of belly dance can be likened to the weaving of a tapestry, in which each thread represents different aspects of our being—physical, emotional, and spiritual—where their intertwining creates a beautiful and cohesive whole. As dancers weave through their routines, they stitch their fragmented selves together into an integrated persona.

Physically, belly dancing enhances flexibility, coordination, and strength, particularly in the core muscles, which are crucial for overall health but often neglected in traditional workouts. The undulating movements improve digestion and boost cardiovascular health by increasing heart rate at a sustainable pace.

On an emotional level, belly dance allows for the expression of feelings through movements that can be both exhilarating and liberating. The rhythms and beats provide an outlet for expressing joy, sorrow, passion, and tranquility—emotions that might be stifled in everyday interactions but can surface and find expression in the dance.

Spiritually, belly dance acts as a meditative practice. The focus required for precise movements draws attention inward toward a deeper understanding of oneself at a soul level. It becomes not just an exercise but a ritual that nourishes the spirit by aligning bodily movements with inner vibrations.

PERSONAL GROWTH OPPORTUNITIES WITHIN BELLY DANCE

Belly dancing offers more than just an opportunity for physical activity—it is a platform for profound personal growth and empowerment. When dancers regularly engage with this art form, they develop not only physical skills but also emotional resilience and spiritual insights.

Each step taken in belly dance could be seen as stepping stones toward greater self-confidence and body positivity. Dancers learn to embrace their bodies regardless of shape or size, celebrating what their bodies can do rather than conforming to external beauty standards. This empowerment fosters greater self-esteem and body acceptance.

The practice of belly dance also cultivates resilience. Learning new choreographies challenges the mind, while perfecting movements demands persistence and patience—qualities that are transferable to other aspects of life. Overcoming these challenges instills a sense of achievement and fortitude.

Moreover, on this journey of personal growth through belly dance, participants often discover hidden facets of their personalities—strengths they didn't know they had or passions previously untapped. This discovery process is empowering as it unlocks new potentials for personal development.

Finding a community that supports and uplifts your belly dance journey is invaluable. Whether it's through classes, workshops, or online forums, being around like-minded individuals who share your passion can significantly enhance your experience.

Belly dancing goes beyond mere movement; it invites each dancer into deeper realms of self-exploration where every step enhances physical prowess while opening doors to emotional healing and spiritual enlightenment—a true embodiment of holistic integration.

Belly dancing serves as a gateway to personal transformation, encompassing body wellness, emotional release, and spiritual connection. As we've seen, belly dance harmonizes and enhances every facet of your life, promising a richer, more balanced existence. It intertwines the physical benefits of movement with emotional liberation through music and the spiritual awakening from connecting deeply with oneself. The dance's fluid movements help to strengthen the body while its rhythmic nature soothes the mind, creating the perfect equilibrium between physical activity and mental peace.

The integration of masculine and feminine energies is central to belly dancing. This dance form encourages you to explore aspects of both strength and grace within yourself, reflecting the balance that many seek in their daily lives. By embracing these dualities, dancers often experience an increase in self-awareness and self-esteem, both of which are crucial for personal empowerment.

Furthermore, belly dance is deeply connected with the activation of energy centers or chakras in the body. Each movement has the potential to open up and balance the chakras, facilitating a smoother flow of energy throughout the body. This not only enhances your physical vitality but also promotes emotional stability and clarity of thought. To truly benefit from belly dancing's potential for transformation, it is essential to engage regularly with its practice. Each session helps elevate one's vibrational frequency, gradually shifting from lower states of negativity to higher planes of positivity such as joy and love. This elevation is not merely about feeling better temporarily; it's about cultivating an enduring state of well-being that permeates all facets of life.

As you continue exploring each movement and melody, remember that you are engaging in a transformative experience that goes beyond mere physical exercise—it is a journey toward a more empowered, balanced, and harmonious life. Embrace this beautiful art form; let it guide you toward deeper connections with yourself and the world around you as you continue on your path to personal fulfillment and well-being.

References:

1. Abrão, A. C. P., & Pedrão, L. J. (2005). The contribution of belly dance to body composition and physical fitness in women. *Journal of Physical Activity and Health*, 2(4), 452-461.
2. Na Nongkhai, M., Muktabhant, B., & Nishio, C. (2014). Effects of Belly Dancing and Nutritional Education on Body Composition and Serum Lipids Profiles of Obese Women in a study at Obesity Clinic Projects at Community Health Center. *Journal of Science and Technology*, 6(2), 1-10.

2
THE DANCE OF ENERGIES

As the sun began its descent below the horizon, its fading light cast elongated shadows over Central Park, where Emma was lost in the rhythms of her belly dancing. The cool evening air carried the scent of hot dogs from nearby food carts and the earthy aroma of the park's lush greenery. In the background, the distant honking of New York City traffic mingled with children's laughter created an urban symphony that harmonized with the Middle Eastern melodies emanating from Emma's portable speaker.

Emma's body swayed and undulated, each movement a testament to the delicate balance between strength and grace that she was seeking to embody. As she danced, her mind wandered to the interplay of feminine and masculine energies within her—a concept she had been exploring deeply through her dance classes at a local studio. Her arms, fluid and graceful, painted intricate patterns in the air, while her hips, strong and grounded, anchored her to the Earth. This dance was a physical representation of the harmony she yearned to achieve in her hectic New York life.

The park buzzed with typical city energy with a golden retriever joyfully barking at a squirrel scampering up an ancient oak tree and an elderly couple strolling hand-in-hand along the winding path. Joggers and cyclists whizzed by with some pausing to watch Emma's mesmerizing movements. These everyday scenes grounded her swirling thoughts, reminding her of life's simpler joys amid the chaos of city living.

Emma paused for a moment, her heart pounding in sync with the rhythmic beats that filled the air. She closed her eyes, feeling the warmth of the fading sun on her skin and the gentle caress of the breeze through her hair. In this moment, she felt a profound connection to the world around her, as if her dance had somehow brought her into alignment with the natural rhythms of life—a stark contrast to the frantic pace of her day job as a marketing executive.

As she resumed dancing, Emma's movements became more intentional, each step and sway a deliberate exploration of the energies within her. She visualized roots growing from the soles of her feet, anchoring her to the earth and drawing up its stabilizing, nurturing energy. At the same time, she imagined a shimmering cord of light extending from the crown of her head, connecting her to the vast expanse of the sky and the limitless potential it represented.

With each movement, Emma felt a shift occurring within her. The tensions and stresses of her daily life—the looming deadlines, the difficult clients, the pressure to keep climbing the corporate ladder—all seemed to melt away, replaced by a growing sense of clarity and purpose. She realized that this dance was more than just a hobby or a form of exercise—it was a tool for self-discovery and transformation.

As the sun finally dipped below the skyline, painting the sky in a breathtaking array of oranges and pinks reflecting off the glass facades of nearby skyscrapers, Emma slowly brought her dance to an end. She stood still for a moment, her body humming with the energy she had cultivated through her movements. A profound sense of peace and contentment washed over her, as if she had tapped into a wellspring of inner strength and wisdom.

Emma gathered her belongings and made her way out of the park, her steps light and purposeful. As she walked, she couldn't help but notice how different she felt compared to when she had arrived at the park straight from the office, tense and frazzled. Now, she felt centered and rejuvenated, ready to face whatever challenges tomorrow might bring.

She knew that her journey with belly dance was far from over—there was still so much to learn, so many layers of herself to uncover. And in this moment, she felt a renewed sense of excitement and dedication to her practice. She made a mental note to sign up for the advanced class her instructor had been encouraging her to try.

As Emma hailed a taxi to take her back to her apartment, she couldn't help but smile. She had set out to find balance and harmony in her life, and through the ancient art of belly dance, she had discovered a path that promised to lead her there. With each sway of her hips and graceful arc of her arms, she was one step closer to becoming the woman she was meant to be—strong, graceful, and in tune with both her feminine and masculine energies.

As the taxi weaved through the bustling streets, Emma found herself looking forward to her next dance session. She realized that this practice was becoming more than just a way to unwind after work—it was a journey of self-discovery that was slowly but surely transforming her life. As the city lights flickered all around, she felt a sense of excitement for what the future held, both on and off the dance floor.

> **Dance is the hidden language of the soul.**
> —Martha Graham

Joany Gauvreau

THE RISE OF FEMININITY: CONNECTING WITH THE DIVINE FEMININE WITHIN

For many women (and men), belly dance serves as a powerful tool for awakening and embracing their feminine energy—the sacred feminine essence that resides within. This connection to the divine feminine is at the heart of Feminicity, a concept that emphasizes the importance of rising feminine energy for personal growth and empowerment.

Scholars and practitioners have long explored the deep connection between belly dance and feminine power. Research in this field highlights how this ancient dance form can awaken and strengthen feminine energy in the body, celebrating the female form and spirit. Numerous studies underscore the transformative potential of belly dance in awakening women to their innate power and creativity.

Feminicity was founded on this very principle—the belief that by reconnecting with the divine feminine through practices such as belly dance, women can tap into a profound source of strength, creativity, and wisdom. This aligns with contemporary perspectives on the transformative power of belly dance and its ability to awaken feminine energy.

Feminine energy, as understood in Feminicity, represents the internal aspect of existence—the energy that has yet to be manifested. It is connected to the primordial source, often described as fluid light or pure being. This energy is oceanic in nature, encompassing everything without differentiation or individualization.

Through the undulating movements and graceful expressions of belly dance, women can embody this archetypal feminine energy, honoring their innate capacity to create, nurture, and transform. This practice becomes a sacred ritual, a way to commune with the inner self and reclaim the power and beauty of the feminine spirit.

As dancers engage with the rhythms and flows of the music, they create a space for feminine energy to rise and flourish. This rising of feminine energy brings with it a sense of empowerment, self-acceptance, and emotional vitality. It allows women to connect with their intuition, their sensuality, and their authentic selves, fostering a deep sense of wholeness and well-being.

In a world that often undervalues feminine qualities, Feminicity offers a sanctuary where women can explore and celebrate their true nature, free from the constraints of society's expectations. This concept aligns with the view of belly dance as a means for women to reclaim their bodies and their sensuality in societies that often deny or suppress these aspects of femininity.

By reconnecting with the divine feminine through ancient art forms like belly dance and various modern practices, women can tap into a profound source of strength, creativity, and wisdom. This connection can potentially lead to personal transformation and a deeper understanding of their feminine power.

BALANCING FEMININE AND MASCULINE ENERGIES: THE PATH TO WHOLENESS

Within each of us resides two fundamental energies: the feminine and the masculine. These energies, often misunderstood as being tied to gender, are actually complementary forces that exist in all individuals, regardless of their gender identity. Understanding and balancing these energies is crucial for personal growth, emotional well-being, and spiritual development.

Feminine Energy: Feminine energy is often associated with the below characteristics:

- Intuition and creativity
- Receptivity and nurturance
- Flexibility and adaptability
- Emotional expressiveness
- Connection to nature and its cycles

This energy is fluid, cyclical, and inward-focused. It's the energy of being, of allowing, and of embracing the present moment. Feminine energy is often likened to water—flowing, adapting, and capable of great power in its flexibility.

Masculine Energy: Masculine energy is typically characterized by the following:

- Logic and analytical thinking
- Action and assertiveness
- Structure and stability
- Focus and direction
- Goal-oriented behavior

This energy is linear, outward-focused, and action-oriented. It's the energy of doing, achieving, and manifesting. Masculine energy can be likened to fire—direct, transformative, and capable of great impact through its focus and intensity.

The Interplay of Energies

These energies are not opposites but complementary aspects of a whole. Just as the concept of the yin and yang in Chinese philosophy represents the interplay of opposite but interdependent forces, feminine and masculine energies work together to create balance and harmony.

In our modern world, there's often an imbalance, with masculine energy overvalued in many societies. This can cause us to be disconnected from our intuitive, receptive sides with an overemphasis on action and achievement at the expense of being and allowing.

Achieving Balance: True wholeness comes from the integration and balance of both feminine and masculine energies. This balance allows us to enact the following in our lives.

- Act decisively while remaining open to intuition
- Pursue goals while staying connected to our emotions
- Provide structure while remaining flexible
- Express strength while embracing vulnerability

Cultivating this balance involves developing an awareness of how these energies manifest within us. It requires a conscious effort to strengthen the underrepresented energy in our lives and to learn how to shift between energies as needed.

Practical Steps for Achieving Balance

1. **Self-reflection:** Regularly check in with yourself to identify which energy is dominant and which needs nurturing.
2. **Mindfulness practices:** Meditation and mindfulness can help you become more aware of your internal energies.
3. **Embodiment exercises:** Physical practices that alternate between fluid, receptive movements and strong, directed actions can help you experience and integrate both energies.
4. **Emotional awareness:** Pay attention to your emotional responses and learn to balance emotional expression with logical thinking.
5. **Connect with nature:** Spending time in nature can help reconnect you with cyclical, feminine energy.
6. **Goal setting with action:** Engaging in focused, goal-oriented activities will help you cultivate masculine energy.

By consciously working to balance these energies, we can achieve a more harmonious state of being. This balance enables us to navigate life's challenges with both resilience and grace, to form deeper connections with others, and to experience a more authentic and fulfilling existence.

Remember, the journey toward achieving balance is ongoing and personal. The key is to approach it with curiosity and compassion, allowing yourself to explore and integrate these fundamental aspects of your being.

ACTIVATING THE CHAKRAS: A JOURNEY THROUGH THE BODY'S ENERGY CENTERS

Belly dance movements can activate and balance other vital energy centers, or chakras, within the body. Each chakra is associated with specific physical, emotional, and spiritual attributes, as well as feminine and masculine energies. Additionally, each chakra is represented by a unique color that carries a specific meaning and vibration. By focusing on these areas during dance and incorporating specific movements, practitioners can experience profound healing, personal growth, and a harmonious balance of energies.

The journey of self-discovery through the chakras is a powerful practice that can be enhanced through dance and movement. Let's explore each chakra, its associated color and meaning, the corresponding belly dance movements, and the feminine and masculine energies associated with each of them.

THE CHAKRA MODEL: CULTIVATING HARMONY THROUGH ACTIVATING KEY RHYTHMIC ALIGNMENTS

The CHAKRA Model stands for Cultivating Harmony Through Activating Key Rhythmic Alignments. This framework is designed to help practitioners engage with the chakra system through the rhythmic and expressive movements of belly dance. By using this model, dancers can activate, align, and balance their chakras, leading to an overall sense of well-being and personal transformation.

Why this Acronym?

1. **Cultivating Harmony:**
   - *Cultivating* implies a deliberate and nurturing process. Just as a gardener tends to a garden, ensuring that each plant receives what it needs to thrive, this model encourages dancers to attentively nourish their minds, bodies, and spirits through targeted practices.
   - *Harmony* is the ultimate goal—creating a balanced state in which the physical, emotional, and spiritual aspects of one's being are in sync. In the context of the chakra system, harmony refers to a balanced flow of energy throughout the body, ensuring that no one chakra is overactive or underactive.

2. **Activating:**
   - *Activating* refers to the process of awakening and energizing the chakras through movement. Each chakra governs specific aspects of our well-being, and by activating them, we stimulate the associated physical, emotional, and spiritual functions.
3. **Key:**
   - *Key* highlights the importance of specific movements and affirmations that target particular chakras. These are not random or general exercises but carefully chosen techniques that align with the unique qualities of each chakra, ensuring a focused and effective practice.
4. **Rhythmic:**
   - *Rhythmic* underscores the significance of rhythm in belly dance. Rhythm is not just a background element but a guiding force that influences how energy flows within the body. The rhythm of the music combined with the rhythm of the movements creates a powerful synergy that enhances the activation and alignment of the chakras.
5. **Alignments:**
   - *Alignments*, in this context, refer to the alignment of the body's energy centers with their optimal states of function. It's about bringing each chakra into alignment with its natural, balanced state, allowing for the free flow of energy and the harmonious integration of mind, body, and spirit.

The Purpose of the CHAKRA Model

The CHAKRA Model serves as a roadmap for integrating the spiritual and physical aspects of belly dance into a unified practice that fosters holistic well-being. By using this model, practitioners can do the following:

- **Target specific energy centers:** Through precise movements and affirmations, dancers can focus on particular chakras that

need attention, whether to activate a dormant energy or to balance an overactive one.
- **Enhance personal transformation:** This model provides a structured approach to using belly dance as a tool for self-discovery, healing, and spiritual growth, ensuring that each session contributes meaningfully to the practitioner's journey.
- **Create a balanced practice:** By addressing each chakra in a methodical way, dancers can create routines that are not only physically enriching but also spiritually and emotionally balanced.

How the CHAKRA Model Works

The CHAKRA Model is designed to be both intuitive and systematic. It encourages practitioners to assess their current energetic state and choose movements and affirmations that will bring them into greater harmony. The model can be used flexibly, allowing dancers to focus on one chakra at a time or to create a full routine that engages all chakras in a balanced manner.

The CHAKRA Model is more than just an acronym; it is a comprehensive approach to using belly dance as a powerful tool for cultivating harmony within oneself. By activating key rhythmic alignments, practitioners can experience profound transformations that resonate through all aspects of their lives, leading to a deeper connection with themselves and the world around them.

EXPLORING EACH CHAKRA

Let's explore each chakra, including its associated color and meaning, the corresponding belly dance movements, the feminine and masculine energies connected with it, and the powerful affirmations that can enhance your practice.

1. **Muladhara (root chakra):**
    - **Color:** Red
    - **Meaning:** Grounding, stability, security, and survival

- **Energy:** Primarily masculine
- **Movements:** Deep hip drops, strong foot patterns, low stances
- **Affirmation:** "I am"
- **Explanation:** The root chakra is about our basic needs and our sense of safety and security. The affirmation "I Am" serves as a powerful declaration of existence, reinforcing one's connection to the earth and the fundamental right to be present in this world. When performing grounding movements, such as deep hip drops and low stances, the focus is on feeling deeply rooted and secure in your body and environment.

2. **Svadhishthana (sacral chakra):**
   - **Color:** Orange
   - **Meaning:** Creativity, sensuality, pleasure, and adaptability
   - **Energy:** Primarily feminine
   - **Movements:** Fluid figure eights, pelvic rolls, flowing arm undulations
   - **Affirmation:** "I feel"
   - **Explanation:** The sacral chakra governs our emotions, sensuality, and creative energy. The affirmation "I feel" acknowledges the right to experience pleasure and emotional depth. As you engage in fluid, sensual movements like figure eights and pelvic rolls, you embrace the flow of your emotions and connect with your creative and sensual nature.

3. **Manipura (solar plexus chakra):**
   - **Color:** Yellow
   - **Meaning:** Personal power, confidence, self-esteem, and willpower
   - **Energy:** Primarily masculine
   - **Movements:** Sharp hip accents, chest lifts, energetic arm gestures
   - **Affirmation:** "I do"
   - **Explanation:** The solar plexus chakra is the center of personal power, confidence, and will. The affirmation "I

do" emphasizes the ability to take decisive action and assert one's will. Through strong, energetic movements such as sharp hip accents and chest lifts, you are cultivating a sense of empowerment and purpose, enhancing your confidence and ability to manifest your desires.

4. **Anahata (heart chakra):**
   - **Color:** Green
   - **Meaning:** Love, compassion, forgiveness, and emotional healing
   - **Energy:** Primarily feminine
   - **Movements:** Chest circles, gentle hip swaying, graceful turns
   - **Affirmation:** "I love"
   - **Explanation:** The heart chakra is the center of love and compassion. The affirmation "I love" strengthens the capacity to give and receive love. As you perform heart-opening movements like chest circles and gentle sways, your focus is on allowing love to flow freely through you, embracing both self-love and compassion for others.

5. **Vishuddha (throat chakra):**
   - **Color:** Blue
   - **Meaning:** Communication, self-expression, creativity, and authenticity
   - **Energy:** Primarily masculine
   - **Movements:** Arm undulations, head slides, improvisational accents
   - **Affirmation:** "I speak"
   - **Explanation:** The throat chakra is linked to communication and self-expression. The affirmation "I speak" encourages the expression of one's truth and creativity. As you explore movements like arm undulations and head slides, your focus is on expressing your authentic self through the dance, using your body as a medium for communication and creativity.

6. **Ajna (third eye chakra):**
   - **Color:** Indigo

- **Meaning:** Intuition, wisdom, imagination, and spiritual insight
- **Energy:** Primarily feminine
- **Movements:** Slow torso figure eights, intuitive arm gestures
- **Affirmation:** "I see"
- **Explanation:** The third eye chakra is the seat of intuition and spiritual insight. The affirmation "I see" enhances your ability to perceive and understand beyond the physical senses. Through slow, deliberate movements like torso figure eights and intuitive gestures, you tap into your inner wisdom and trust your intuitive abilities, allowing them to guide your dance.

7. **Sahasrara (crown chakra):**
   - **Color:** Violet or White
   - **Meaning:** Spiritual connection, enlightenment, and unity consciousness
   - **Energy:** Integration of feminine and masculine
   - **Movements:** Ecstatic upper body undulations, joyful spins
   - **Affirmation:** "I understand"
   - **Explanation:** The crown chakra represents spiritual connection and enlightenment. The affirmation "I understand" reflects a deep comprehension of the interconnectedness of all things. As you engage in movements like ecstatic undulations and joyful spins, feel your connection to the divine and the universe while embracing a sense of unity and spiritual fulfillment.

IMPLEMENTING THE CHAKRA MODEL

The CHAKRA Model provides a structured yet flexible framework for creating balanced routines that incorporate movements targeting each chakra while embodying both feminine and masculine qualities. This approach allows dancers to cultivate a deeper sense of harmony and connection within themselves, as well as a greater capacity to navigate life's challenges.

Practitioners are encouraged to assess their current energetic state and adjust their practice accordingly. For example, focusing on root and solar plexus chakra movements can help restore stability and personal power when feeling ungrounded. Emphasizing sacral and heart chakra movements can promote creativity and emotional connection.

Remember that this practice is a personal and intuitive process. Trust your body's wisdom and allow movements to flow organically, guided by your inner experience and breath. By integrating the CHAKRA Model into your belly dance practice, you can unlock a powerful tool for self-discovery, healing, and transformation.

As you explore the chakras through dance, you're not only activating and balancing your energy centers but also cultivating a profound connection to your authentic self. Embrace this journey of self-exploration and allow the ancient wisdom of the chakras to guide you toward a deeper understanding of yourself and the world around you.

To deepen your exploration of feminine/masculine energies and chakras in belly dance, I've included a special addendum at the end of this book, "Guide to Movements and Music for Elemental Energies, Feminine/Masculine Balance, and Chakra Activation," which offers specific dance movements, music recommendations, and practice tips. It's designed to help you embody these concepts in your dance practice. I encourage you to use this resource as you continue your journey, allowing it to enrich your understanding and experience of these powerful energetic principles.

3

ANATOMIC HARMONY: THE BODY'S SYMPHONY

Emily, a dedicated physical therapist, found herself drawn to the allure of belly dancing. One warm evening, she mustered the courage to step into a local dance studio, her heart racing with a mix of anticipation and trepidation. The studio welcomed her with a warm ambiance, its walls adorned with vibrant tapestries and the air filled with the enchanting melodies of Middle Eastern music. As Emily joined the other students, she couldn't help but feel a twinge of self-doubt. Would she be able to keep up with the more experienced dancers?

As the class began, the instructor's calm yet authoritative voice guided everyone through the warm-up exercises. Emily listened intently; her therapist's mind fascinated by the instructor's explanations of the muscle groups involved in each movement.

The undulations and isolations were unlike anything Emily had ever experienced. She felt her core muscles engage in new ways, burning with exertion but also excitement. As they progressed to chest circles and arm movements, Emily marveled at the amount of strength and control required.

The hip movements proved to be a formidable challenge. Emily's legs trembled as she attempted hip drops, shimmies, and figure eights. But the instructor's patient guidance and encouragement helped her persist. By the time they reached footwork and turns, Emily was flushed from exertion but exhilarated. She felt a profound connection to her body, a harmonious symphony of muscles and joints working together. As she twirled across the floor, a sense of liberation washed over her.

In the weeks that followed, Emily became a devoted student of belly dance. She absorbed every bit of knowledge, from the intricate muscle interplay to the cultural significance of the dance. But more than that, she discovered a part of herself she had never known existed.

Through belly dance, Emily found a unique form of self-expression. She connected to her femininity and strength in ways she hadn't before. The studio became more than just a place to dance; it became a sanctuary where she found a supportive community of women who celebrated their bodies and abilities.

As Emily's confidence grew, so did her grace and poise. She stood taller, moved with more fluidity, and radiated a newfound self-assurance. Belly dance had transcended being just a hobby or exercise; it had become an integral part of her life. Reflecting on her journey, Emily realized that belly dance had taught her far more than just dance moves. It had shown her the incredible adaptability of the human body, the power of a shared passion, and the joy of embracing one's authentic self.

Each time Emily stepped onto the dance floor, she felt a profound sense of gratitude. She had discovered her path to physical and emotional harmony, a journey that celebrated the magnificent capabilities of the human body. With every sway and shimmy, she reveled in the beautiful synthesis of art and anatomy that belly dance embodies.

> **The body says what words cannot.**
> **—Martha Graham**

DISCOVERING ANATOMIC HARMONY THROUGH THE SYMPHONY OF BELLY DANCE

Imagine your body as a grand orchestra, each muscle and joint an instrument playing in perfect harmony. This is the essence of belly dance—a mesmerizing art form that transforms your anatomy into a living, breathing symphony. As we explore the intricate world of belly dance, prepare to be amazed by your body's hidden capabilities.

The Core: Igniting the Fire Within

In the world of belly dance, your body becomes a living, breathing work of art. Imagine your upper body as a graceful hot-air balloon, filled with lightness and possibility. Your solar plexus, just below your ribcage, is the source of an inner fire—a wellspring of energy and creativity that fuels your dance. As you move, the fire in your solar plexus radiates warmth and vitality throughout your body. It energizes your core muscles—the rectus abdominis, obliques, and transverse abdominis, which work in harmony to create the mesmerizing undulations and resonance that define belly dance. Although we do work in isolating the body parts, the overall effect is one of fluid connection and synergy.

Below, your pelvis serves as the sturdy basket of this imaginary hot-air balloon. It grounds you, providing a stable base from which all movements originate. While dancing, you feel the interplay between the airy lightness of your upper body, the fiery energy of your core, and the solid foundation of your pelvis.

The Spine: A Pillar of Strength and Flexibility

Your spine is the central axis of this hot-air balloon, connecting the airy upper body to the grounded pelvis. Each undulation and roll of your torso activates the intricate muscles supporting and moving your spine. From the cervical spine in your neck to the lumbar spine in your lower back, belly dance movements promote a full range of motion and encourage a proper alignment.

The Pelvis: A Cradle of Creation and Expression

The pelvis, your balloon's basket, is a central focus in belly dance, often associated with creativity and emotional expression. Through the fluid, circular movements of the hips and lower abdomen, you'll tap into your primal energy, unleashing a powerful force of healing and transformation.

The Fascia: Weaving a Web of Connectivity

Beneath your skin lies the fascia, a hidden network of connective tissue. Think of it as the intricate ropes and netting of your hot-air balloon, crucial to belly dancing. As you move through undulating and spiraling patterns, you are gently creating tension and release in this fascial network, promoting flexibility and whole-body integration.

Practical Belly Dance Exercises[1]

1. **Core strengthening:** Master belly rolls and undulations by engaging your abdominal muscles in a wavelike motion. Visualize stoking the fire in your solar plexus.
2. **Back flexibility:** Practice snake arms and gentle torso movements to increase flexibility and strength in your back muscles. Imagine your spine as the central pole of your balloon, flexing and extending with grace.
3. **Hip stability:** Engage in hip drops, shimmies, and figure eights to strengthen your hip muscles. Feel the stability of your pelvis as the balloon's basket.
4. **Leg and foot agility:** Perform a variety of foot patterns to improve leg strength and foot agility. These can include grapevines, small

---

[1] For visual demonstrations of these exercises and more, you can find free videos on my YouTube channel: @femonlinedance.

steps with hip accentuation, or any combination of steps that feel comfortable and engaging.
5. **Upper body alignment:** Practice shoulder shimmies, arm waves, and head slides for proper alignment and flexibility. Envision the lightness of your upper body as the balloon itself.

UNLOCK THE SYMPHONY WITHIN: HARMONIZING BODY AND SPIRIT THROUGH DANCE

Belly dance is more than just a physical art form; it's a holistic practice that engages multiple body systems in a harmonious symphony of movements. It's a dance that speaks to your musculoskeletal system, fascia network, and even your glands, promoting a unique physical harmony that enhances flexibility, strength, and overall vitality.

ACTIVATING THE SENSES FOR EMOTIONAL AND SPIRITUAL WELL-BEING

Belly dance engages all your senses, creating a profound state of presence and vitality. From the scent of incense grounding you while the rhythmic music guides your movements, to the visual splendor of the dance itself, each sense contributes to a holistic experience that transcends the physical. This multisensory engagement is a powerful assertion of your personal sovereignty, allowing you to fully inhabit your body and make conscious choices about how you experience and interact with your environment.

As you continue your journey into belly dance, remember that you're not just learning steps; you're unlocking the symphony within. You're discovering the dancer that's been waiting to emerge, telling your unique story through movement. Embrace the image of the hot-air balloon—let your upper body float with grace, stoke the fire in your core, and stay grounded through your pelvis. Welcome to the transformative power of belly dance, where anatomy becomes art and your body becomes a masterpiece in motion, a living expression of your sovereignty.

4
RHYTHMS OF THE SOUL

As the muezzin's call to prayer faded into the bustling activity of Cairo's streets, Zara stood alone in her modest apartment. The setting sun cast long shadows across the room, its golden light filtering through the intricate patterns of her grandmother's lace curtains. The air was heavy with the mingled scents of cardamom from her cooling tea and jasmine wafting up from the market below.

Zara, a thirty-three-year-old journalist, found herself at a crossroads. By day, she wrote for a well-known newspaper, fulfilling her family's expectations of a "respectable" career. But as twilight descended, she became something her parents would never approve of—an aspiring belly dancer.

With trembling hands, Zara reached for her phone, rereading the message that had thrown her ordered world into disarray. An invitation to perform at an upcoming cultural festival—a dream come true, yet a potential nightmare for her family's reputation. Her finger hovered over the "accept" button, her heart pounding with both excitement and anxiety. As if on cue, the old radio on her dresser crackled to life, filling the room with the haunting melodies of Umm Kulthum's "Enta Omri." Zara closed her eyes, allowing the music to wash over her. Almost unconsciously, her hips began to sway, her body responding to the rhythm as naturally as breathing.

The movement transported her back to her childhood, to secret moments shared with her mother in this very room. She remembered watching in awe as her mother danced, her face a canvas of emotions—joy, sorrow, longing—all expressed through the undulation of her body. "This is our heritage, habibti," her mother had whispered, eyes shining. It was a conversation between body and soul, telling stories that words could not capture.

But those moments were rare, stolen in the absence of Zara's father and brothers. As she grew older, the weight of societal expectations pressed down on her. "Nice girls don't dance like that," her aunt had scolded when she caught Zara mimicking her mother's movements. "You'll bring shame to the family." The memory sent a pang through Zara's heart. She thought of her cousin Fatima, whose dreams of becoming a professional dancer had been crushed under the weight of family honor. Fatima now lived a quiet life as a housewife, her passion reduced to secret shimmies while doing housework.

Zara's own journey into belly dance had been fraught with challenges. She'd started with online videos, practicing in secret, terrified of being discovered. It wasn't until university that she found the courage to attend a class, telling her parents she was in a study group. The first time she felt the vibration of the doumbek drum beneath her feet and saw her reflection in the studio mirror moving in perfect synchronicity with the music, she knew she had found her calling.

Now as the rhythms of the darbuka drums joined Umm Kulthum's voice, Zara's movements grew bolder. Her hips traced fluid figure eights, her arms undulating like desert snakes. In the dance, she found liberation. Here, she wasn't bound by the constraints of society or family expectations. Here, she could express every facet of her being—strength and vulnerability, joy and sorrow, tradition and modernity.

As she danced, Zara felt a deep connection not just to her own body but to generations of women before her as well. She thought of the pharaonic temples where ancient dancers had performed sacred rituals, of the nineteenth-century ghawazee who had danced in the streets of Cairo, of her grandmother who had whispered tales of secret dance gatherings where women celebrated life's milestones together.

The music shifted, and Zara recognized the distinctive rhythm of the maqsoum. She adjusted her movements, feeling the accent on the second beat guide her hips in sharp, precise motions. She marveled at how each rhythm seemed to evoke a different emotion, a different aspect of her personality.

As she moved, Zara reflected on the rich tapestry of Arabic music that formed the backbone of belly dance. She had spent countless hours studying the various maqamat—the melodic modes that gave Arabic music its distinctive sound and emotional depth. The current piece was in Maqam Rast, its joyful, uplifting tones filling her with a sense of celebration and hope.

But with each shimmy and undulation, doubt crept in like a shadow. What would her colleagues at the newspaper think if they knew? Would she be taken seriously as a journalist if word got out about her dancing? And her family—the thought of their disappointment and anger made her stomach churn. Breathless, Zara paused by the open window, gazing out at the glittering lights of Cairo. The city was changing, she knew. Young women like her friend Nour were taking belly dance classes at modern studios, calling it a celebration of their heritage and a form of exercise. But for every step forward, there seemed to be a pushback. Just last month, a well-known dancer was arrested for "inciting debauchery" with her social media videos.

As the final notes of the song faded away, Zara realized that her cheeks were wet with tears. The dance had unlocked something within – a deep yearning to be true to herself, to honor both her passion and her heritage. She thought of recent studies she'd read about dance's ability to reduce stress, enhance cognitive function, and strengthen cultural identity. Could she use her skills as a journalist to change perceptions, to reclaim belly dance as the art form it truly was?

Zara recalled a podcast she had recently discovered, *Spotlight Sessions*, that featured an interview with Sarah Thompson, CEO of Rehabilitative Rhythms. Thompson, a music therapist, discussed how music therapy can help people with neurological impairments and developmental differences improve their quality of life. This scientific approach to music therapy resonated deeply with Zara's personal experience—the way the intricate rhythms and haunting melodies of Arabic music seemed to reach into her very soul, helping her process emotions she couldn't even name.

She thought about the concept of *tarab*—the state of ecstasy that could be reached through music and dance. It was more than just enjoyment; it was a transcendent experience, a way of connecting with something greater than oneself. Zara had experienced glimpses of tarab during her dance practice, moments when the boundary between herself and the music seemed to dissolve, leaving only pure expression.

The festival invitation still glowed on her phone screen. Accepting would mean stepping out of the shadows, risking everything she had worked for. But declining would be to deny a fundamental part of herself. With a deep breath, Zara picked up her phone. Whatever she decided, she knew that the rhythm of the dance would continue to beat within her, a pulse connecting her to a lineage of strong, expressive women. In that moment, she felt that somehow, someday, she would find a way to bridge the worlds within her, to be both the respected journalist and the passionate dancer, honoring her family's values while being true to her spirit.

As she stood poised between decision and indecision, the night air carried the faint sounds of music from a distant celebration. Zara closed her eyes, allowing herself to imagine a future in which her two worlds could coexist—where the ancient rhythms of belly dance could harmonize with the beat of modern Cairo. With trembling fingers, she began to type her response, ready to take the first step toward a new, uncertain, thrilling journey.

In that moment, Zara embodied the essence of belly dance—a beautiful fusion of tradition and modernity, of personal expression and cultural heritage. Her journey reflected the transformative power of this ancient art form, and its ability to heal, empower, and connect. As she embraced the rhythms of her soul, Zara was not just dancing but reclaiming her heritage, one shimmy at a time.

> Music produces a kind of pleasure which
> human nature cannot do without.
> —Confucius

UNLEASH THE SYMPHONY WITHIN: HARNESSING MUSIC FOR WHOLENESS

Surrendering to the seductive rhythms of belly dance music opens us to a profound journey of emotional healing. The pulsing beats of the doumbek, the haunting melodies of the ney, and the shimmering accents of the zils—each sound has the power to evoke and transform our innermost feelings.

Science has long recognized the therapeutic benefits of music and rhythmic movement. Immersing ourselves in the sonic landscape of belly dance engages not only our bodies but also our brains and nervous systems. The repetitive, entrancing rhythms can induce a state of relaxation and receptivity, allowing us to access and release stored emotions and traumas.

Different musical styles and instruments create specific emotional atmospheres, from the primal, grounding energy of tribal drums to the sensual, fluid expression of classical Middle Eastern melodies. By attuning ourselves to these varied soundscapes, we can explore the full spectrum of our emotional experience, finding joy as well as deep soul nourishment in the dance.

THE RHYTHMIC SYNERGY OF MOVEMENT AND MUSIC

At the core of belly dance lies a rhythmic synergy between movement and music—a dynamic interplay that is more than mere performance art. It is a powerful medium for holistic self-exploration and healing. In belly dance, music does not simply accompany movement; it enhances, guides, and transforms it. The intricate rhythms and melodies serve as a transformative force. They not only provide a backdrop for physical movement but resonate more deeply, influencing emotional states and energy levels as well. As dancers move to these sounds, they experience a unique form of nonverbal communication that connects them with their innermost selves.

The emotional resonance of belly dance music is palpable. Each beat can elevate or soothe the dancer's mood, acting as an auditory guide through varied emotional landscapes. By aligning movements with specific musical elements—rhythms, tempo, and melody—dancers are embarking on a journey that can lead them to profound emotional insights and energetic transformations.

EMBRACE YOUR INNER RHYTHM: A JOURNEY INTO THE RICHNESS OF ARABIC MUSIC

Arabic music is at the heart of belly dance, much like jazz music being essential to swing dance. Both genres rely on intricate rhythms and melodies that deeply influence dance movements. Understanding Arabic music can significantly enhance your belly dance experience by making it more expressive and emotionally resonant. As someone who is not a musician but is always learning, I've found that you don't need to be a musical expert to connect with and appreciate this rich tradition. What's most important is how the music makes you feel and how it moves you.

Arabic music features unique elements such as maqamat (melodic modes) and tarab (musical ecstasy). Maqamat are like the scales used in Western music but with distinct emotional qualities and structures. Tarab refers to the deep emotional connection and ecstasy experienced while listening to the music, similar to the euphoria felt during an intense jazz improvisation.

To start your journey into Arabic music, immerse yourself in different types of belly dance music. Here are a few songs to begin with:

1. "Enta Omri" by Umm Kulthum: A classic song that showcases the deep emotions and expressive power of Arabic music.

2. "Kifak Inta" by Fairuz: This song exemplifies tarab with Fairuz's emotive vocal delivery. It's a perfect example of how Arabic music can convey complex emotions and create a profound connection with the audience.

As you listen to these songs, don't worry about analyzing them technically. Instead, focus on how they make you feel and how your body wants to move in response. This intuitive approach is just as valid and meaningful as any technical understanding.

MUSIC AS YOUR DANCE PARTNER

In belly dance, music is not just background noise; it actively shapes and guides your movements. Think of the music as your partner, helping you to express emotions and tell a story through dance. Even without formal musical training, you can develop a deep, instinctive connection to the rhythms and melodies that will inform and enhance your dance.

While understanding the basics of maqamat and its rhythms can be helpful, it's not necessary to fully enjoy and express the music. Trust your intuition and let the music guide you. Here are some common rhythms you might encounter, described in terms of how they might feel rather than in technical musical terms:

1. A steady, grounding beat that makes you want to step firmly and confidently (like the maqsoum rhythm).
2. A bouncy, playful rhythm that inspires quick, light movements (similar to the saidi rhythm).
3. A rolling, flowing rhythm that encourages a continuous, wavelike motion (akin to the chiftetelli rhythm).

MINDFULNESS IN BELLY DANCE

Developing mindfulness through belly dance is another critical aspect. It involves deepening one's mental awareness during each movement by focusing on bodily sensations and breath patterns in sync with the music. This practice not only improves the dancer's technique but also enriches their spiritual life by fostering a heightened state of presence and awareness.

Incorporate mindfulness practices into your routine by focusing on bodily sensations as you move. Try synchronizing your breath with rhythmic patterns in the music for a deeper immersion. For example, with a steady rhythm, try inhaling deeply for four counts and exhaling for the next four counts. This practice helps you stay present while enhancing the fluidity and expressiveness of your movements, even if you're not counting beats in a technical way.

PRACTICAL STEPS TO HARNESS MUSIC FOR WHOLENESS

1. **Engage with different musical styles:** Listen to various styles of belly dance music to gain an understanding of the range of emotional atmospheres they create. Notice how tribal drums make you feel grounded, while classical Middle Eastern melodies invite fluidity and sensuality.
2. **Align movements with music:** Practice aligning your dance movements with the rhythms, tempo, and melodies of the music. Start with simple steps and gradually incorporate more complex combinations as you become more comfortable.
3. **Focus on emotional expression:** Use the music to guide your emotional expression in dance. Let each beat and melody inform your movements, creating a dialogue between your inner emotions and the external soundscape.
4. **Cultivate mindfulness:** Pay close attention to how your body feels as you move. Synchronize your breath with the music's rhythm to deepen your connection to the dance and enhance your presence.
5. **Explore improvisation:** Allow the music to inspire spontaneous movements. Trust your instincts and let your body respond naturally to the sounds to foster a unique and personal dance experience.

CREATING YOUR DANCE PLAYLIST

Develop a personalized playlist that resonates deeply with you and evokes specific moods or energy levels during practice sessions. Regularly update and refine this playlist as your musical tastes evolve. Here are some suggestions:

1. "Leylet Hob" by Umm Kulthum: A classic love song that evokes deep emotions and passion.
2. "El-Tannoura" by Fares Karam: An upbeat, joyful piece that energizes and uplifts.
3. "Hobbo Ganna" by Sherine: An expressive and powerful piece that showcases Sherine's vocal abilities and emotional depth, inviting introspection and self-expression.

As you listen to these songs, focus on how they make you feel and how they inspire your movements. Your emotional response to the music is your most valuable guide in creating a meaningful dance experience.

RESOURCES FOR DEEPENING YOUR MUSICAL JOURNEY

While our intuitive connection to the music is paramount in belly dance, some dancers may wish to deepen their understanding of Arabic music. For those interested in exploring further, here are some valuable resources:

1. **Online platforms:**
   - www.georgedimitrisawa.com: This website offers a wealth of information about Arabic music theory, maqamat, and rhythms. It features articles, lessons, and audio examples that can enhance your understanding of the musical structure behind belly dance.
   - MaqamWorld: An excellent resource for those curious about the intricacies of maqamat. It provides detailed explanations,

audio samples, and even interactive tools to help you recognize different maqamats.
  - o Darbuka Rhythms: This site focuses on Middle Eastern percussion, offering insights into the various rhythms used in belly dance music.
2. **Books and music collections:**
  - o *The Art of the Early Egyptian Qanun* by George Dimitri Sawa: This two-volume book delves into the history, theory, and practice of the Middle Eastern zither. While it's an academic work, it provides fascinating insights into Arabic musical traditions.
  - o *The Rough Guide to Bellydance* (music compilation): This diverse collection of belly dance music from various regions and styles is an excellent way to expose yourself to a range of maqamat and rhythms.
3. **Workshops and classes:** Consider attending workshops or classes focused on Arabic music appreciation for dancers. Many belly dance festivals and conferences offer sessions on music theory and interpretation, which can deepen your understanding and enhance your dance practice.
4. **Collaborations with musicians:** If possible, try to occasionally dance with live musicians. This experience can provide invaluable insights into how the music is created and how dancers and musicians interact.

Remember, while these resources can enrich your understanding, they are not necessary for enjoying and expressing yourself through belly dance. The most important thing is to listen deeply, feel the music, and let it move you.

INTEGRATING MUSIC INTO YOUR DAILY LIFE

To truly immerse yourself in the world of belly dance music, consider incorporating it into your daily routine. Listen to Arabic and Middle

Eastern music while doing chores, during your commute, or as you relax in the evening. This consistent exposure will help you internalize the rhythms and melodies, making them feel more natural when you dance. You might find yourself unconsciously moving to the music as you go about your day—a shimmy while washing dishes, or a hip drop while waiting in line. Embrace these moments! They're signs that the music is becoming a part of you, even if you're not formally studying it.

CONCLUSION: YOUR UNIQUE MUSICAL JOURNEY

As we conclude this chapter on harnessing music for wholeness in belly dance, remember that your journey with the music is uniquely yours. Whether you choose to delve into the technical aspects of Arabic music or prefer to connect with it purely on an emotional and intuitive level, what matters most is the joy, healing, and self-expression you find in the dance.

The rich tapestry of belly dance music offers endless opportunities for exploration and growth. As you continue to dance, you'll develop a deeper connection to the rhythms, melodies, and emotional landscapes of the music. This connection will inform and enhance your movements, allowing you to express yourself more fully and authentically through dance.

Embrace the power of music in your belly dance practice. Let it guide you, move you, and transform you. Through this beautiful synergy of sound and movement, you'll discover new depths of emotional expression, physical awareness, and spiritual connection. Your dance will become not just a performance but a profound journey of self-discovery and wholeness.

5

UNVEILING THE DANCE WITHIN

In the soft glow of early evening, Rachel stood at the edge of her small town's community center, her heart pounding with a mixture of anticipation and anxiety. The faint strains of Middle Eastern music drifted through the air, beckoning her towards the dance studio where a beginner's belly dance class was about to start. Rachel's fingers nervously traced the cross pendant hanging around her neck, a reminder of the conservative Christian upbringing that had shaped her beliefs about dance and self-expression.

Rachel's journey to this moment had been a long and conflicted one. Growing up in a tight-knit evangelical community, she had been taught that dancing, especially sensual forms like belly dance, was a gateway to temptation and sin. Church socials were limited to modest group dances, and any form of movement that drew attention to the body was strongly discouraged.

Despite these deeply ingrained beliefs, Rachel found herself inexplicably drawn to the art of belly dance. She had stumbled upon a video of a performance online, and the fluid movements and joyful expression of the dancer had captivated her in a way she had never experienced before. The dance seemed to awaken something deep within, a longing for self-expression and freedom that had been suppressed by years of conditioning.

As Rachel hesitated at the threshold of the studio, every step felt like a rebellion against her upbringing. She realized how much she had changed since that first encounter with belly dance—not just in her perception of movement but in her understanding of herself. The very act of signing up for this class had been a declaration of independence, a step toward reclaiming her right to explore and express herself fully.

Taking a deep breath, Rachel stepped into the studio. The room was filled with women of all ages and body types, some looking as nervous as she, others chatting excitedly. The instructor, a woman with kind eyes and a welcoming smile, greeted Rachel warmly.

As the class began, Rachel felt a mix of exhilaration and guilt. Each movement, from the basic hip circles to the fluid arm patterns, felt both foreign and strangely familiar. It was as if her body had been waiting for this moment, ready to speak a language that it had always known but had never been allowed to use.

Throughout the class, Rachel grappled with an internal conflict, the one between her desire to embrace this new form of expression and the voices of her upbringing warning her of its dangers. She found herself alternating between moments of pure joy as she lost herself in the music and movements, and pangs of shame as she imagined what her family and church community would think if they could see her now.

As the class progressed, Rachel began to question the belief that dancing was inherently sinful. She looked around at her classmates, seeing not temptresses or sinners but women of all backgrounds coming together to celebrate the beauty and strength of their bodies. There was a sense of community and support in the room that reminded her of the best aspects of her church experience but without the judgment or restrictions.

After class, Rachel lingered, her body humming with newfound energy. The teacher approached her, sensing perhaps the internal struggle Rachel was experiencing. "How did you find your first class?" she asked gently.

Rachel hesitated, then let the words tumble out. "It was ... incredible. But I'm struggling. I was raised to believe that this kind of dance is wrong, sinful even. But it felt so ... right. So freeing."

The teacher nodded understandingly. "Many women come to belly dance with similar concerns, but this dance is about so much more than what it might appear on the surface. It's about connecting with your body, expressing your emotions, and finding strength and confidence in yourself. There's nothing sinful about that."

In the weeks that followed, Rachel continued to attend classes, each session bringing new challenges and revelations. She delved into the history and cultural significance of belly dance, learning about its roots in Middle Eastern and North African traditions. This knowledge helped her appreciate the depth and complexity of the dance beyond the stereotypes she had been taught.

Rachel also found herself part of a supportive community of dancers who understood her struggles. Many shared similar stories of overcoming religious or cultural taboos surrounding dance. Their encouragement and shared experiences helped Rachel navigate her own journey of self-discovery and acceptance.

As her skills improved, so did Rachel's confidence. She began to see her body not as a source of temptation or shame but as a beautiful instrument capable of creating art. The dance became a form of moving meditation, allowing her to process emotions while connecting with a sense of spirituality that felt more authentic and personal than anything she had experienced before.

Rachel's transformation didn't go unnoticed by her family and community. While some reacted with concern or disapproval, others were intrigued by the positive changes they saw in her. She found herself having deep, sometimes difficult conversations about faith, body autonomy, and the nature of sin and virtue. These discussions challenged her to articulate her evolving beliefs and to stand firm in her newfound convictions.

As she continued on her belly dance journey, Rachel began to see how the practice aligned with, rather than contradicted, her core values of compassion, community, and celebrating the divine. She started to view her body as a temple in a new light—not as something to be hidden away but as a sacred vessel through which she could express joy, gratitude, and worship.

Rachel's story is a testament to the transformative power of belly dance, especially for those coming from conservative or restrictive backgrounds. Through dance, she found a path to self-acceptance, body positivity, and a more inclusive and compassionate worldview. Her journey reminds us that true faith and spirituality can be enhanced, not diminished, by embracing the full spectrum of human expression and creativity.

As Rachel continued to dance, she became an inspiration to others in her community who were struggling with similar conflicts involving their upbringing and their desire for self-expression. She began to see that her journey was not just about personal growth but also about opening doors for others to explore their own paths to authenticity and joy.

In the undulating rhythms of belly dance, Rachel had found more than just a new hobby—she had discovered a way to reclaim her body, her spirituality, and her sense of self. And with each shimmy and sway, she moved closer to the woman she was always meant to be: strong, free, and unafraid to dance to the rhythm of her own heart.

Dance is the fastest, most direct route to the truth.
—Gabrielle Roth

SHEDDING THE SHADOWS: EMBRACING THE LIGHT OF BELLY DANCE

For many individuals raised in conservative traditions, the journey of belly dance is not only a path of physical and emotional healing but also a powerful tool for releasing shame, fear, and the self-doubt associated with the act of dancing itself. In the safe, supportive space of the dance floor, they can begin to shed the layers of conditioning that may have long held them back from fully expressing themselves.

Creating a nurturing environment is key to this process of unveiling. When dancers feel seen, accepted, and celebrated in their dance community, they gain the courage to explore their vulnerabilities, challenging deeply ingrained beliefs about the sinfulness of dancing. They learn to trust the wisdom of their bodies, to honor their own unique rhythms and ways of moving, and to embrace dance as a sacred and transformative practice.

Through the gentle yet powerful practice of belly dance, countless individuals from conservative backgrounds have reclaimed their sense of self-worth, their joy, and their resilience. They have found solace in the company of other dancers who understand the challenges and triumphs of overcoming conditioning. And they have emerged from the dance stronger, more compassionate, and more fully alive than ever before.

STEPS TO EMBRACING YOUR DANCE JOURNEY

1. **Identify misconceptions:** Begin by examining your preconceived notions about belly dance. Write down any negative associations or fears you may have. Are these based on fact or cultural stereotypes? Research the origins of these ideas and challenge them with accurate information about the dance's history and purpose.
2. **Cultural education:** Immerse yourself in the rich cultural tapestry of belly dance. Study its origins in Middle Eastern and North African cultures. Learn about the different styles, from Egyptian and Turkish to Tribal Fusion. Explore the traditional music, costumes, and cultural contexts in which belly dance flourishes. This knowledge will deepen your appreciation and respect for the art form.
3. **Challenge your conditioning:** Confront the societal and religious expectations that may have limited your self-expression. Question why certain movements are considered "inappropriate" in your culture. Practice gentle self-talk to counteract negative thoughts about your body or the act of dancing. Remind yourself that dance is a natural, joyful form of human expression.
4. **Celebrate individuality:** Embrace your unique body type and natural movement style. Experiment with different belly dance moves to find what feels most comfortable and authentic to you.

Remember that there's no "perfect" belly dancer body—the dance is for everyone. Celebrate the ways your personal history and experiences inform your dance.

5. **Find your tribe:** Seek out supportive belly dance communities, both locally and online. Attend classes, workshops, and performances. Join social media groups and forums dedicated to belly dance. Cultivate friendships with fellow dancers who understand your journey. Having a supportive community can provide encouragement, inspiration, and valuable feedback.
6. **Foster self-compassion:** Be patient and kind to yourself as you learn. Acknowledge that mastering any new skill takes time. Celebrate small victories, like learning a new move or performing your first choreography. When you make mistakes or feel discouraged, treat yourself with the same compassion you'd offer a friend.
7. **Empower yourself through expression:** Use belly dance as a tool for emotional expression and personal growth. Allow yourself to feel empowered by the movements. Connect with the music and let it guide your body. Use dance as a form of moving meditation, focusing on the present moment and the sensations in your body. Let go of self-consciousness and dance for your own joy and satisfaction.
8. **Educate others:** As you grow in your practice, become an ambassador for belly dance. Share your experiences with friends and family. Dispel myths and misconceptions when you encounter them. Consider organizing performances or workshops to introduce others to the art form. By educating others, you not only spread appreciation for belly dance but also reinforce your own understanding and commitment to the practice.

UNRAVELING THE MISCONCEPTIONS AND FEARS SURROUNDING BELLY DANCE

Despite its enchanting nature, belly dance is often misunderstood, viewed by some as merely exotic entertainment. This narrow perception overlooks the dance's rich cultural heritage and its significant benefits, such as enhanced fitness, emotional expression, and spiritual connection.

Delving into the essence of belly dance reveals its capacity as a powerful tool for personal growth and healing. By engaging in this ancient practice, dancers tap into primal energies that dissolve fears and foster well-being. The dance acts as a mirror, reflecting not just the physical form but also the emotional landscape of the dancer.

Unfortunately, many potential dancers hesitate, held back by fears of judgment or feelings of inadequacy. The inherent vulnerability in dancing, which requires an openness to self-discovery and public observation, can be daunting. It's essential to recognize that this vulnerability is where transformation thrives—it's the fertile ground for genuine personal growth.

Concerns about cultural sensitivity also arise, with dancers worrying about the potential to misappropriate or disrespect the origins of belly dance. While it's crucial to approach the dance with respect for its traditions, embracing its evolution demonstrates the adaptability and continuing relevance of belly dance. Fusion styles, like Tribal Fusion or Bollywood Belly Dance, honor the dance's heritage while reflecting the diversity of its current practitioners.

CULTIVATING EMPOWERMENT THROUGH SELF-EXPRESSION

Belly dance transcends a mere sequence of steps by blossoming into an expressive dialogue between the body and the drumbeats. Each movement shape—from fluid undulations to sharp shimmies, from circular hip rotations to linear arm pathways—weaves a story of reclaiming one's body, mind, and spirit. The interplay of curved and straight lines, the contrast between soft flows and staccato accents, all contribute to this rich vocabulary of motion. This art form serves as a profound vehicle for empowerment, particularly for those from conservative backgrounds in which dancing might be viewed with skepticism or outright prohibition. Through these diverse movement shapes, dancers find a voice that speaks volumes without uttering a word, challenging societal norms and celebrating the beauty of self-expression.

Each step in belly dance symbolizes an affirmation of strength and fluidity, striking a delicate balance between meticulous control and a graceful surrender to the rhythm. This balance mirrors life's own ebb and flow, teaching dancers resilience through flexibility, both physically and in navigating the complexities of societal norms.

Regular engagement in belly dance not only builds physical strength but also fosters emotional resilience, aiding practitioners in other areas of their life. Moreover, the discipline required to master intricate movements enhances mindfulness, calming the mind and providing a refuge from the struggles between personal desires and external expectations.

During this journey, dancers frequently experience moments of deep connection with themselves—instances of spiritual alignment brought forth by rhythmic motion. These moments are illuminating, shedding light on previously hidden facets of personality and revealing inner strengths that were perhaps obscured by years of conditioning.

By understanding misconceptions, overcoming personal insecurities, and embracing self-expression in belly dance, individuals can unlock powerful avenues for personal transformation—balancing body rhythms with life's melodies for a holistic sense of well-being. Belly dance acts as a conduit for harmonizing the sacred feminine and masculine energies within. This integration aligns with the principles of chakra alignment discussed in previous chapters.

Each movement in belly dance can be viewed as a dynamic interplay of these energies, promoting not only physical alignment but also spiritual and emotional balance. The fluid motions help unlock the flow of energy through the chakras, enhancing personal power and fostering a deeper connection to the spiritual self.

As dancers continue their journey, they realize that overcoming misconceptions and fears about belly dance is not just about changing how they dance; it's about transforming how they live. Each step taken is a step toward reclaiming power over one's body and narrative. Recognizing and dismantling limiting beliefs allows practitioners to embrace the true essence of belly dance, unlocking a profound source of empowerment and self-expression.

This transformative journey of belly dance encourages each dancer to let every shimmy, undulation, and spin celebrate the sacred feminine and masculine energies that reside within. As dancers continue to harmonize these forces through movement, they become part of a global community of individuals who are reclaiming their power and awakening to the beauty, resilience, and boundless creativity of the human spirit.

This dance is not merely an act of physical expression but also a profound spiritual practice that echoes the ancient rhythms of our ancestors, inviting every dancer to explore the depths of their being and celebrate their inherent worth. Through the experiences of countless individuals, we see how belly dance can be a powerful catalyst for personal growth, healing, and transformation, helping practitioners to shed the shadows of limiting beliefs and step into the light of their true, radiant selves.

6

THE INNER DANCE OF DISCOVERY

In the soft glow of early evening, Jacqueline stood alone in her studio, her feet bare against the cool wooden floor. At sixty-five, she exuded a vitality that defied outdated notions of aging. As the sun dipped low, casting long shadows through the windows, a gentle breeze whispered through, carrying the faint scent of pine from the nearby forests of the small nickel-mining town in Ontario, Canada.

Jacqueline embodied the essence of a "queenager," a term celebrating women over forty-five who redefine midlife with confidence, vitality, and purpose. As she gazed at her reflection in the mirror, she marveled at the radiant, self-assured dancer staring back at her. Her silver hair shimmered in the fading light, a crown of both wisdom and beauty.

Her journey to this moment had been transformative. At fifty, weighing 250 pounds, Jacqueline had taken her first belly dance class. Over the years, as she fell deeply in love with the dance, she shed one hundred pounds, finding not just physical health but a profound joy in movement. Her passion grew so strong that she even crafted her own dance costumes, each stitch a testament to her dedication. At sixty, filled with a desire to share the life-changing power of belly dance, Jacqueline made the decision to become a teacher herself.

As she prepared for her evening class, Jacqueline reflected on the inspiring community of mature dancers she had become a part of. Her thoughts drifted to the legendary figures who had shaped her journey and the world of belly dance. She drew inspiration from a diverse group of renowned belly dancers, each with their own unique wisdom and contributions to the art form.

These dancers, ranging in age from their fifties to nineties, included luminaries like Dina, Amani, Fifi Abdou, Carolina Varga Dinicu (nicknamed "Morocco"), Princess Farhana, Aziza, Jillina Carlano, and Carolina Nericcio. Their collective wisdom emphasized that belly dance is a lifelong journey of growth, self-discovery, and expression. They taught Jacqueline about the importance of connecting with one's body and soul, embracing passion and joy in dance, while viewing advancing age as an opportunity for deeper expression rather than a limitation.

As her students began to arrive, filling the studio with excited chatter, Jacqueline felt a surge of gratitude. She was part of this vibrant tapestry of women redefining aging through the art of belly dance. Each shimmy, each undulation, each moment of connection with the music was an act of joyful defiance against society's limited expectations of older women.

Jacqueline took a deep breath, centering herself before the class began. She knew that tonight, as every night, she would be doing more than teaching dance steps. She would be guiding these women on a journey of self-discovery, empowerment, and transformation.

As the first notes of music filled the air, Jacqueline smiled, ready to lead her students in this timeless dance of femininity, strength, and ageless beauty. She began the class with a gentle warm-up, encouraging her students to focus on their breath and become present in their bodies.

"Ladies," Jacqueline addressed her class, "as we dance tonight, I want you to focus on the present moment. Feel the music in your bones, the earth beneath your feet, the air on your skin. This is your time to be fully present in your body."

As they moved through the choreography, Jacqueline watched her students transform. Women who had entered the studio with slumped shoulders and tired eyes now stood tall, their faces alight with joy and confidence. She saw reflections of her own journey in each of them, the initial hesitation, the gradual awakening, and finally, the blossoming of self-assurance and grace.

The concept of queenagers, as exemplified by Jacqueline and these inspiring dancers, aligns with contemporary research on aging and vitality. Recent studies in gerontology have consistently shown that maintaining an active lifestyle, pursuing new interests, and engaging in social activities can contribute to better physical and mental health outcomes for older adults.

Moreover, many health organizations worldwide now emphasize the importance of challenging ageist stereotypes and promoting active, engaged lifestyles for older adults. Activities like belly dance, with their emphasis on movement, self-expression, and community, are increasingly recognized as valuable for healthy aging.

As the class progressed, Jacqueline guided her students through the principles of body awareness, vulnerability, and self-compassion. She encouraged them to listen to their bodies, to embrace the emotions that come up while dancing, and to treat themselves with kindness and understanding.

"Remember," she told them, "belly dance is not about perfection. It's about expression, connection, and joy. Allow yourself to be vulnerable, to make mistakes, and to grow. This is how we transform not just our bodies but our spirits as well."

The alchemy of movement and music in belly dancing acts as a purifying outlet for emotional release, transforming everyday stress into a vibrant energy that rejuvenates the spirit. Jacqueline watched as her students found balance between structure and freedom, between strength and softness, mirroring the essential balance required in life.

As the class drew to a close, Jacqueline led her students in a cool-down stretch, encouraging them to reflect on their experience. The studio was filled with a palpable sense of accomplishment and sisterhood.

For Jacqueline and her students, belly dance is not just a dance but a way of life—a celebration of the feminine divine, a path to physical and emotional healing, and a source of endless joy and vitality. It is a powerful testament to the fact that women can continue to grow, learn, and thrive at any age.

As the last student left the studio, Jacqueline took a moment to herself. She closed her eyes, feeling the lingering energy of the class, the echo of the music in her body. She felt grateful for this journey, for the transformative power of belly dance, and for the community of strong, vibrant women she is privileged to guide and learn from.

In the quiet of the empty studio, Jacqueline began dancing, her body moving instinctively to an internal rhythm. In this moment, she was ageless, timeless, a woman in her prime, embracing the joy of movement and the endless possibilities that lay ahead.

> **I see dance being used as communication between body and soul, to express what is too deep for words.**
> **—Ruth St. Denis**

UNLOCKING THE ESSENCE OF TRANSFORMATION THROUGH ANCIENT RHYTHMS

As we embark on the path of belly dance, we discover that this journey is not only about mastering choreography or perfecting techniques; it is an invitation to cultivate a profound sense of mindfulness and presence in our lives. With each breath, each movement, each beat of the music, we have an opportunity to awaken to the richness of the present moment and to the subtle sensations and insights that arise within.

Incorporating the practice of mindfulness into our dance sessions can deepen the process of inner discovery. By bringing our full attention to the flow of our breath, the placement of our feet, the graceful arc of our arms, we are training ourselves to be more attuned to the language of our bodies and hearts. We learn to move not just with external precision but with internal awareness and intention as well.

Regular engagement with belly dance as a mindfulness practice can have far-reaching benefits for our mental and emotional well-being. As we develop the capacity to witness our thoughts and feelings with greater clarity and compassion, we may find ourselves better equipped to navigate the challenges of daily life with grace and resilience. Our belly dancing becomes not just a form of self-expression but a pathway to greater self-understanding and inner peace.

The keys to unlocking this transformative power are body awareness, vulnerability, and self-compassion. These elements, when cultivated through disciplined practice and cultural immersion, are foundational pillars that can significantly enhance one's experience and personal growth.

Belly dance demands a heightened sense of one's physicality and the subtle energies that flow through the body. This acute awareness allows dancers to move with precision and grace, transforming simple gestures into expressions of deeper emotional states and stories. It isn't merely about mastering movements; it's about listening to the language of your body and responding in kind.

Vulnerability in belly dance acts as a gateway to authenticity. As dancers expose their emotional core through performance, they connect more deeply with themselves and their audience. This openness can be daunting but it's essential for genuine expression. Embracing vulnerability paves the way for a transformative experience that transcends mere performance, touching the depths of the human experience.

Self-compassion is crucial as it encourages dancers to accept their journey, missteps and achievements alike. In belly dance, as in life, perfection is not the goal—expression is. Self-compassion fosters patience and love of oneself during the learning process, promoting resilience and a positive mindset, which are necessary for growth.

CULTIVATING BODY AWARENESS, VULNERABILITY, AND SELF-COMPASSION

The first step in this dance of discovery is cultivating body awareness. As you learn to move your hips and shoulders rhythmically, you are also tuning into subtler bodily signals—the tension in your muscles, the alignment of your spine, and the rhythm of your breathing. This heightened awareness brings a deeper connection to your physical self, which is essential for both dance and daily life.

Imagine belly dance as a mirror reflecting not just your physical form but also the state of your mind and emotions. Each movement and posture reveals layers of how you feel about yourself. It's here, in the gentle sway of a hip circle or the bold sharpness of a shimmy, where vulnerability begins to surface. Engaging in these movements exposes personal insecurities but also paves the way for embracing them with compassion.

Developing self-compassion through belly dance involves acknowledging that missteps are part of learning—not just in dance but in life. When a dancer stumbles over a complex beat, the reaction shouldn't be a harsh self-critique but rather an understanding smile and an encouraging nod to try again. This practice teaches patience and kindness toward oneself, which are critical components of growth.

The practice of belly dance intertwines various aspects of ourselves. Body awareness leads to recognizing vulnerabilities, which when embraced with compassion, enhances personal transformation. Each session is an opportunity to not only refine your dance technique but to also cultivate a more forgiving and understanding relationship with yourself.

THE IMPORTANCE OF REGULAR PRACTICE AND CULTURAL IMMERSION

To truly master belly dancing, regular practice is indispensable. Just as a musician must practice scales daily to refine their artistry, a belly dancer must consistently engage with the basic movements and rhythms to build their fluency in the language of dance. This repetition solidifies muscle memory and deepens emotional expression through movement.

But beyond mere practice lies the rich tapestry of cultural history that belly dance offers. Immersing oneself in the origins and traditions of this ancient art form adds depth and authenticity to one's performance. Understanding the cultural significance behind each gesture and step enriches the dancer's expressiveness and connection to the dance.

Consider regular practice as watering a plant; it's essential for growth. Similarly, cultural immersion is like sunlight—necessary for blossoming fully. Together, they nourish the dancer's skill and soul, enabling not only technical proficiency but also a heartfelt embodiment of the spirit of the dance.

Engaging regularly with experienced teachers can accelerate this growth process. These mentors provide insights into both technique and the subtle nuances that make belly dance so captivating. They act as guides through which dancers can navigate their own pathway toward mastery while staying true to the dance's cultural roots.

Through consistent practice intertwined with cultural learning, dancers find themselves not just performing steps but telling stories with their bodies—stories woven from threads of ancient traditions and personal emotion.

APPROACHING BELLY DANCE WITH AN OPEN HEART

Approaching belly dance with an open heart is crucial for experiencing its full transformative power. This openness allows dancers to fully embrace the new challenges and experiences that come with learning such an intricate art form.

Imagine each step in belly dancing as planting seeds in fertile soil—the more open-hearted you are, the deeper the seeds can root, allowing for richer growths of skill and emotion. This approach not only enhances technical ability but also deepens the emotional engagement with each movement.

When dancers allow themselves to experience each vibration and rhythm without reservation or judgment, they tap into profound levels of self-expression. It becomes less about getting the steps right and more about what those steps represent on a deeper emotional or spiritual level.

The real beauty emerges when dancers connect their movements to their breaths—each inhale preparing for motion; each exhale executed with grace. Such synchronization between body movement and breath exemplifies how open-heartedness manifests physically within the realm of belly dancing.

By embracing vulnerability while performing or in practice sessions—perhaps facing fears of inadequacy or judgment—dancers can overcome barriers that may otherwise hinder their artistic expression.

An open heart not only enriches one's performance but catalyzes profound personal transformations by weaving together heightened body awareness, embraced vulnerabilities, nurtured compassion toward oneself, and consistent practice enriched by cultural insights—all culminating in a powerful journey toward holistic well-being.

THE ALCHEMY OF MOVEMENT AND MUSIC

The alchemy of movement and music in belly dancing acts as a purifying outlet for emotional release, transforming everyday stress into a vibrant energy that rejuvenates the spirit. The dance serves as a dynamic expression of life's balance—between structure through choreography and freedom through improvisation. Such balance is crucial in navigating the complexities of daily life.

Moreover, integrating feminine and masculine energies within the dance mirrors the essential balance required in life. This integration empowers individuals to express strength and softness simultaneously, promoting a harmonious existence both on and off the dance floor.

Understanding how the movements in belly dance can influence our chakras reveals another layer of its transformative power. These movements do more than strengthen muscles; they enhance our vibrational frequency and help align our energy centers, facilitating a healthier, more balanced state of being.

Finally, remember that each step taken in belly dance is not just a move but an opportunity to connect with ancient rhythms that heal, empower, and transform. As you continue your journey in belly dance, let these insights guide you toward a deeper self-awareness and a more joyful expression. Embrace each moment in your dance as an opportunity for personal alchemy, transforming every challenge into a step forward in your journey of self-discovery.

By cultivating body awareness, vulnerability, and self-compassion, dancers unlock a pathway to not only enhanced physical health but also emotional and spiritual well-being.

EMBRACE THE JOURNEY

Regular practice is the backbone of mastery in belly dance. It solidifies the technical skills while deepening the emotional connection with each movement. Cultural immersion enriches this practice, providing a deeper understanding and appreciation of the dance's origins, thus adding layers of authenticity and meaning to your personal experience.

Approaching belly dance with an open heart allows for transformative experiences that can significantly impact one's life. It is through this openness that dancers can fully embrace the vulnerabilities and strengths revealed through each motion. This enhances personal expression while fostering a profound connection with oneself and the community.

As Jacqueline found, the journey of belly dance is one of continuous growth and discovery, transcending age and defying limitations. It is a celebration of life, an exploration of self, and a testament to the endless possibilities that dance offers. Let each step, each movement, and each moment in your practice be a reminder of the incredible journey you are on—a journey that embraces transformation, celebrates individuality, and honors the timeless art of belly dance.

7

EMBODYING THE ELEMENTS

Suzy stood poised, her bare feet firmly rooted on the smooth wooden floor beneath her. The air in the dimly lit Cairo studio carried the delicate aroma of frankincense and myrrh. Mingling with the distant sounds of the city's bustling streets just beyond these walls—a gentle hum that faded into the background as she closed her eyes and surrendered to the music.

At thirty-eight, Suzy had traveled from her small hometown in Michigan to Egypt, fleeing the aftermath of a painful divorce and the loss of her tech startup. For years, she had poured herself into building a life that looked perfect on paper but left her feeling hollow inside. The collapse of her marriage and business had been devastating, but it also freed her to pursue a long-buried passion: belly dance.

She'd discovered belly dance in her twenties, attending a local class on a whim. The way the dance made her feel—powerful, sensual, and connected to her body—had been transformative. But life, with its demands and expectations, had pulled her away. Now, standing in this sacred space in Cairo, she felt a sense of coming home to herself, of reclaiming a part of her soul that she'd nearly forgotten.

The haunting melodies of the ney flute ushered in a sense of veillike fluidity, each note seeming to ripple through her like water caressing a shoreline. As the rhythms of the riq and daf drums joined in, Suzy felt her body instinctively respond, her movements ebbing and flowing in sync with ancient cadences. This was belly dance in its purest form—a celebration of the elements that sustain all life, and a welcome balm to her wounded spirit.

With each movement, Suzy felt a deep connection to generations of women who had danced before her. She wasn't just performing; she was channeling the wisdom of the ages, allowing it to flow through her and bring healing to her soul.

Suzy began her dance by grounding herself in the earth element. She felt the solid support of the floor beneath her feet as she moved through grounded, steady hip drops. Each movement connected her to the earth's feminine energy, drawing nourishment and stability. The masculine energy of the earth gave her the strength and resilience to maintain her stance, balancing the dual energies within her root chakra. As she danced, Suzy felt the weight of her past failures and heartbreaks melting away, replaced by a newfound sense of belonging and purpose.

Transitioning to the water element, Suzy moved through undulations and figure eights, feeling her sacral chakra come alive. The feminine energy of water brought a sense of emotional depth and intuition, while the masculine energy of adaptability allowed her to seamlessly transition between movements, reflecting the ever-changing nature of water. She thought of the mighty Nile, its life-giving waters mirrored in her fluid movements, and felt a deep connection to the land that had called her here. In these movements, she found the flexibility to adapt to her new life, to flow around obstacles rather than break against them.

Next, she tapped into the fire element with sharp accents and percussive shimmies. The fire's transformative energy activated her solar plexus chakra. The masculine energy of action and strength merged with the feminine energy of passionate creativity, allowing her to move with intensity and purpose. Suzy channeled the fierce determination that had brought her halfway across the world to pursue her dream, feeling the power of her transformation with each sharp movement. In the fire, she found the courage to forge a new path, to rise from the ashes of her old life like a phoenix reborn.

Finally, Suzy's graceful arm patterns and flowing turns brought the air element to life. Her heart chakra opened to the expansive, liberating energy of air. The masculine energy of clarity and perspective combined with the feminine energy of intuition and spiritual connection allowed her to soar and expand her dance to new heights. As she spun, Suzy felt a profound sense of freedom, realizing that in this moment, she was exactly where she was meant to be. The air element brought with it a new vision for her future—one in which she could share the healing power of this dance with others who, like her, were seeking to rebuild their lives.

In this sacred space, Suzy embodied the harmonious dance of the elements, finding true beauty, expression, and mastery in her movements. As the music faded, she stood still, breathing deeply, feeling more alive and connected than ever before. This wasn't just a dance practice; it was a journey of self-discovery, a path to healing, and a connection to something far greater than herself. In the alchemy of the elements, Suzy had found not just a new passion but a new purpose—and the strength to embrace whatever challenges lay ahead.

> **Dance is the only art of which we ourselves
> are the stuff of which it is made.**
> **—Ted Shawn**

Joany Gauvreau

DANCING WITH THE RHYTHMS OF NATURE: ELEMENTAL ALCHEMY IN BELLY DANCE

In the rich tapestry of belly dance, the four elements—earth, water, fire, and air—offer us a powerful framework for exploring the full spectrum of our being. By embodying the qualities of each element through specific movements and energetic intentions, we can tap into the elemental forces that shape both our inner and outer worlds. Each element carries aspects of feminine and masculine energies, as well as connections to the chakras, creating a holistic dance experience.

As we learn to dance with the elements, we discover how to bring greater balance and harmony to our lives. We can draw upon the qualities of each element as needed, whether we seek the grounding of earth, the adaptability of water, the passion of fire, or the liberation of air. The dance becomes a way to align ourselves with the natural rhythms and cycles of the universe, finding our place in the great web of life.

The Earth Element: Grounding and Stability

The grounded, rooted energy of the earth can be expressed through deep, solid movements like hip drops and earthy shimmies. By connecting with the stability and nourishment of the earth element, we cultivate a sense of inner strength, of being grounded, and of self-trust. Earth energy is inherently feminine, associated with nurturing and support, and is connected to the root chakra (Muladhara). This chakra governs our sense of security and grounding.

Dance Movements:

- **Hip drops:** Anchor yourself firmly to the ground with each drop, feeling connected to the earth. Imagine your body sinking roots deep into the ground, drawing strength and stability.
- **Earthy shimmies:** Let the vibrations travel up through your legs, reinforcing your rootedness. Visualize the energy of the earth rising through your body, stabilizing and nourishing you.

Additional Details:

- **Music and rhythm:** Deep, resonant drum beats will enhance your feeling of being grounded. Instruments like the dumbek or djembe can provide the earthy vibrations that resonate with the root chakra.
- **Visualization:** Picture yourself as a strong, ancient tree with roots extending deep into the earth. This image can help you feel more connected and grounded during your dance.
- **Affirmation:** "When I connect with the earth element, I feel a deep sense of belonging. It's as if the wisdom of my ancestors flows through me, grounding me in my cultural heritage."

The Water Element: Fluidity and Grace

Just as water molds itself around any vessel, the fluid movements of belly dance adapt effortlessly to the rhythm and melody of the music. The graceful flow of these movements captures the essence of water's energy, blending feminine receptivity and adaptability, associated with the sacral chakra (Svadhisthana), which governs creativity and emotional flow.

Dance Movements:

- **Undulations:** Mimic the gentle waves of the ocean, letting your torso ripple smoothly. Feel the fluidity in your spine and torso, allowing your movements to flow like water.
- **Figure eights:** Create continuous, flowing shapes with your hips, embodying water's adaptability. Imagine drawing endless figures of eight in the air with your hips, flowing seamlessly from one movement to the next.

Additional Details:

- **Music and rhythm:** Flowing, melodic music with instruments like the accordion or the qanun can evoke feelings of flowing water. Slow, continuous rhythms can help you connect with the fluidity of the water element.

- **Visualization:** Picture yourself as a river, flowing effortlessly around obstacles, always in motion yet deeply connected to the source. This can enhance your sense of fluidity and grace.
- **Cultural context:** In many Middle Eastern cultures, water is seen as a symbol of purification and renewal. The fluidity of belly dance movements often mirrors the importance of water in desert regions, where it's seen as precious and life-giving.

The Fire Element: Passion and Intensity

If water symbolizes fluidity, then fire represents passion and intensity. Styles such as drum solos, Latin dance fusion, and flamenco embody this blazing spirit, combining fierce staccato movements with compelling rhythms. Fire energy is masculine, linked to action and transformation, and is connected to the solar plexus chakra (Manipura), the center of personal power and confidence.

Dance Movements:

- **Sharp hip accents:** Use quick, decisive movements to channel fiery energy. Each accent should feel like a spark igniting within, full of power and intensity.
- **Fast shimmies:** Build heat and intensity, radiating outward from your core. Imagine the flames dancing around you, fueled by your inner fire.

Additional Details:

- **Music and rhythm:** Fast-paced, percussive music with strong drumbeats can help you connect with the fire element. Instruments like the tabla or cajón can provide the fiery rhythm needed for these movements.
- **Visualization:** Visualize yourself as a flame, burning brightly and transforming everything it touches. This can help you embody the passion and intensity of fire in your dance.

- **Personal Anecdote:** As a dancer, I've found that connecting with the fire element has helped me overcome stage fright. By channeling that fierce energy, I'm able to transform my anxiety into a powerful, confident performance.

The Air Element: Freedom and Expansion

Finally, the air element symbolizes freedom and expansion. Styles like dervish, veil dance, and waltz capture this airy essence with sweeping arm movements and graceful spins. Air energy is masculine, representing clarity and liberation, and is connected to the heart chakra (Anahata), which balances love and compassion.

Dance Movements:

- **Arm patterns:** Extend your arms in fluid, expansive movements, feeling the freedom of air. Imagine your arms as wings, lifting you higher with each graceful sweep.
- **Spins:** Release yourself into the music, allowing the air to lift you up. Feel the lightness and freedom as you spin, expanding your energy outward.

Additional Details:

- **Music and rhythm:** Light, airy music with instruments like the flute or harp can enhance the feeling of expansion. Rhythms that evoke a sense of flight and freedom can be particularly effective.
- **Visualization:** Picture yourself as a bird soaring high in the sky, free and unencumbered. This can help you connect with the expansive energy of air.
- **Guided meditation:** Before dancing with the air element, try this brief meditation. Close your eyes and take deep breaths. Imagine with each inhale that you're drawing in clear, pure air, filling your entire being with light. As you exhale, visualize any

tension or heaviness leaving your body, allowing you to feel lighter and more expansive.

As we embody these elements while dancing, we begin to realize a profound truth about our own nature. Our bodies are not separate from these primal forces—we are, in fact, made of them.

Consider this: approximately 20–25 percent of our body is earth—our bones and solid tissues. Water makes up about 70 percent of our being. The air we breathe and the spaces within our cells are essential to our existence. And fire is present in every cell, in the form of our metabolic processes and the energy we derive from the sun.

But what if we were to remove these elements? Where would we be? The answer is both simple and profound—we would be everywhere and in everything. We are the universe itself, temporarily taking the form of an individual.

This realization can be transformative, especially for those struggling with body image and self-worth. When we understand that our bodies are literally made of stardust, that we contain elements from distant stars and ancient suns, how can we not see ourselves as magnificent, divine beings?

In belly dance, as we move through the elements—grounding like earth, flowing like water, igniting like fire, and floating like air—we are not just imitating these forces. We are awakening to our true nature as embodiments of the entire cosmos. Each undulation, each shimmy, each graceful arm movement becomes a celebration of our inherent divinity.

So the next time you dance, remember that you are not just a body moving to music. You are the universe in motion, expressing itself through the ancient and sacred language of dance. In this realization lies true freedom, joy, and self-acceptance—the very essence of what belly dance offers to those who embrace it.

THE HARMONIOUS DANCE OF THE ELEMENTS

In the end, true mastery lies in the ability to embody all four elements—earth, water, fire, and air—in perfect harmony. Just as life depends on the delicate balance of these primal forces, so, too, does the art of dance thrive when we embrace their diverse yet interconnected energies.

As you move through each style and each choreography, allow yourself to be grounded to the earth, flow like water, ignite like fire, and soar like the air. Let the elements guide your movements, infusing each step with their ancient wisdom and primal power. Earth grounds you with stability, water nurtures your emotional flow, fire ignites your passion, and air lifts you into an expansive freedom. Embrace the freedom of improvisation, letting your body respond intuitively to the music and the moment.

INCORPORATING ELEMENTAL AWARENESS IN DAILY LIFE

- **Earth:** Practice standing barefoot on natural ground to feel grounded and connected.
- **Water:** Take time to observe bodies of water, noticing their constant flow and adaptability.
- **Fire:** Engage in regular activities that ignite your passion and creativity.
- **Air:** Practice deep breathing exercises to clear your mind and gain new perspectives.

For it is in the harmonious dance of these elemental forces that we find true beauty, true expression, and true mastery of sacred art forms. Embrace the elements, and you embrace the very essence of life itself, pulsing and swirling through your body with each undulation, each shimmy, each breath.

In that moment, you become one with the dance, one with the universe, and one with the eternal rhythm that beats within us all.

To explore the elements further in your dance practice, refer to the addendum at the end of this book, which includes specific movements, music suggestions, and practice tips for embodying each element—earth, water, fire, and air—in your belly dance. This resource will help you deepen your connection to these elemental energies, enhancing your dance and personal transformation.

8

RECLAIMING YOUR LIFE'S RHYTHM

In the soft glow of a late morning, Sarah stood alone in her living room, her feet bare against the plush carpet. The sun streamed through the sheer curtains, casting a warm, gentle light throughout the room. It had been six months since her mastectomy, and the weight of her cancer journey still hung heavily on her shoulders.

Sarah's battle with breast cancer began in the spring of 2018 when a routine self-examination revealed a small, unfamiliar lump. At forty-two, the Denver native had always prided herself on her healthy lifestyle, making the diagnosis all the more shocking. The whirlwind of tests, biopsies, and consultations that followed confirmed her worst fears. The treatment plan was aggressive—a double mastectomy, followed by six rounds of chemotherapy and a year of targeted therapy.

Though the surgeries and treatments had been successful in eradicating the cancer, Sarah felt like a mere shadow of herself, her body and spirit bearing the scars of battle. Her once-vibrant auburn hair was just starting to grow back, a constant reminder of all that she had endured.

As she stood in the living room, memories of her life before cancer drifted through her mind. She thought back to the joy and liberation she had once found in belly dancing classes at her local community center.

The ancient rhythms had stirred a fire within, providing a weekly escape from her demanding job as a high school counselor. The physical and emotional toll of her cancer journey had extinguished that flame, leaving her feeling disconnected and numb.

Sarah closed her eyes, the faint echoes of a Middle Eastern melody playing in her mind—a song from her favorite instructor, Yasmin. Slowly, tentatively, she began to move, her hips swaying to the imagined beat. As the music grew louder in her mind, her movements became more fluid and expressive. Each roll of her abdomen, each shimmy of her shoulders felt like a conversation between her body and her inner self. The dance became a meditation, a way to reconnect with the essence of who she was beneath the layers of pain and fear.

As she lost herself in the imaginary music, Sarah recalled the articles she had read during her recovery—studies that highlighted the profound benefits of belly dancing for cancer survivors. The research showed that this ancient art form could not only help rebuild physical strength and flexibility but also foster a deeper sense of self-acceptance and body positivity. She understood on a profound level now how the dance could be a catalyst for healing and transformation.

With each movement, Sarah felt a renewed sense of connection to her body. She began to see herself not as a collection of scars and losses but as a living, breathing testament to the power of resilience. The dance became a celebration of her strength, a way to honor the journey that had brought her to this moment.

As the weeks passed, Sarah's impromptu living room dance sessions became a daily ritual, a way to reconnect with herself and her body. However, she still hesitated to return to her old belly dance class at the community center, feeling self-conscious about her changed body and uncertain of her abilities.

One day, gathering her courage, she decided it was time to reach out to Yasmin. To her surprise and relief, Yasmin welcomed her back with open arms, assuring her that the class would be a supportive environment for her healing journey.

With trepidation and excitement, Sarah returned to Yasmin's belly dance class at the community center. Though initially nervous about dancing with others, she was met with overwhelming support from her classmates. Many of the women shared their own stories of overcoming personal challenges through dance, creating a powerful sense of community and shared strength.

As Sarah continued her transformative journey through belly dance, both at home and in class, she discovered the power of gratitude in amplifying her healing process. By actively acknowledging and appreciating the positive changes in her life, including a renewed sense of connectedness to her body, her increased strength and vitality, and the supportive dance community she had rediscovered, she was able to cultivate a deeper sense of joy and fulfillment.

Sarah realized that by expressing gratitude for the lessons and blessings along her path, it helped reinforce the growth she had experienced. It also created a positive feedback loop that propelled her forward on her journey of self-discovery and empowerment. She began keeping a gratitude journal, making daily notes of the small victories and moments of beauty she'd encountered.

With each class, Sarah felt more like herself again. The rhythm of the drums echoed the beating of her heart, strong and steady. The fluid movements of her arms and torso reminded her of the resilience and adaptability of her spirit. And in the moments when she caught a glimpse of herself in the studio mirror, she no longer saw just a cancer survivor—she saw a dancer, a warrior, a woman reclaiming her joy and rhythm of her life.

> **There is a vitality, a life force, an energy, a quickening that is translated through you into action, and because there is only one of you in all time, this expression is unique. And if you block it, it will never exist through any other medium and will be lost.**
> **—Martha Graham**

UNLEASH YOUR TRUE POTENTIAL: THE TRANSFORMATIVE POWER OF BELLY DANCE

The healing power of dance and movement, recognized for centuries across diverse cultures, has gained scientific backing, underscoring its therapeutic benefits for various physical and emotional challenges. Research has shown that regular dance activity can significantly decrease symptoms of depression and anxiety (Koch et al., 2019), enhance cardiovascular health (Rodrigues-Krause et al., 2016), boost immune function (Fong Yan et al., 2021), and potentially slow the progression of neurodegenerative diseases like Parkinson's and Alzheimer's (McNeely et al., 2015; Lazarou et al., 2017).

Belly dance, in particular, is noted for its unique amalgamation of physical exercise, rhythmic stimulation, and emotional expression, making it an especially effective form of movement therapy. A study by Bräuninger (2012) found that dance movement therapy significantly improved quality of life and reduced stress levels in participants. Regarding belly dance specifically, research by Moe (2012) highlighted its potential for promoting body appreciation and self-empowerment among women.

For those recovering from illness, injury, or stress, belly dance offers a vibrant pathway back to vitality and a zest for life. This dance form does more than restore physical function; it reconnects participants with the inherent healing capabilities of their bodies, fostering resilience and encouraging growth and transformation. As practitioners engage with belly dance, they tap into the balancing energies of the elements—earth grounds them, water flows through their movements, fire ignites passion, and air lifts them toward freedom.

Integrating belly dance with a holistic wellness routine—alongside balanced nutrition, adequate rest, and effective stress management—creates a robust foundation for lasting health and well-being. Engaging with experienced teachers and a community of fellow dancers provides essential support, offering motivation, inspiration, and a shared journey.

At its heart, belly dance is a profound exploration of the physical, emotional, and spiritual layers of the self. Dancers often embark on a transformative journey toward greater self-awareness and holistic health. The rhythmic movements, synchronized with music, establish a therapeutic space that nurtures the soul, elevating belly dance from a mere physical activity to a spiritual undertaking.

This transformative potential of belly dance is greatly enhanced by its ability to release stagnant emotions and foster personal growth. The interplay between body and music allows for deep self-expression and an emotional release. This helps dancers break through emotional blockages, which enhances their emotional well-being. Regular dance practice shifts vibrational frequencies from lower states of negativity to higher planes of positivity such as joy and love, cultivating a persistent state of well-being.

UNDERSTANDING BELLY DANCE'S ROLE IN EMOTIONAL HEALING AND SPIRITUAL AWAKENING

Belly dance offers a powerful avenue for body reclamation, particularly for those who have experienced physical changes due to illness or surgery. This gentle yet expressive art form enhances proprioception, allowing individuals to reconnect with their bodies in a nurturing way. Unlike high-impact exercises, belly dance provides a gradual return to physical activity, making it ideal for those in recovery.

Regular dance practice shifts the focus from physical limitations to a celebration of the body's capabilities, fostering a positive body image and honoring resilience. This perspective can be transformative for those grappling with body-related challenges.

Beyond its physical benefits, belly dance serves as a conduit for emotional healing and spiritual growth. Its rhythmic movements, reminiscent of ocean waves, can help process suppressed emotions in a supportive environment. The dance stimulates serotonin production in the brain, elevating mood while reducing stress through its meditative qualities.

Rooted in spiritual traditions, belly dance often facilitates transcendental experiences, connecting practitioners to a higher consciousness. Many dancers find that it aligns and balances their chakras, harmonizing their feminine and masculine energies.

Through belly dance, individuals can embark on a holistic journey of physical rehabilitation, emotional release, and spiritual awakening, rediscovering and embracing their bodies with newfound appreciation and joy.

EMOTIONAL AND SPIRITUAL DIMENSIONS OF MOVEMENT

The emotional and spiritual aspects of belly dance play a significant role in healing. The rhythmic movements facilitate a release of trapped emotions, particularly those stored in the hips and abdomen—areas often affected by stress and trauma. This somatic processing allows practitioners to work through deep-seated feelings that may have been holding them back.

The focus required in belly dance serves as a form of moving meditation, promoting mindfulness and present-moment awareness. This mindful movement helps break free of worries about the future or regrets about the past, allowing individuals to fully inhabit their bodies in the present moment.

Many practitioners report feeling their energy centers rebalanced through regular dance practice. While not scientifically proven, this sense of energetic alignment can contribute to an overall feeling of well-being and wholeness.

INTEGRATING BELLY DANCE INTO HOLISTIC RECOVERY

Belly dance complements other aspects of recovery and wellness. Certain movements can enhance physical therapy exercises, improving flexibility and strength in areas weakened by illness or inactivity. The mind-body connection fostered by the dance bridges the gap between physical rehabilitation and psychological healing.

Interestingly, many practitioners notice that increased body awareness leads to more mindful eating habits. They find themselves naturally drawn to more nourishing foods that support their overall health, illustrating how belly dance can indirectly support nutrition and well-being.

EMBRACING BELLY DANCE FOR HOLISTIC WELL-BEING AND A TRANSFORMATIVE JOURNEY

The holistic impact extends into mental health by fostering self-esteem through the mastery of complex choreographies that offer both mental challenges and a sense of accomplishment once the skills are acquired or improved upon.

To illustrate this transformative process using an analogy, consider belly dancing like gardening—through consistent care (practice) and nurturing (self-expression), we cultivate beautiful flowers (skills) that enhance our entire garden (life). Thus, each step taken in learning this dance not only improves technique but enriches life itself at every level.

By embracing belly dance, we engage in a holistic approach to wellness that transforms our physical health while enriching our emotional lives and uplifting our spirits—truly a journey worth embarking upon for anyone seeking fulfillment from within.

To truly integrate these benefits into your life, consider incorporating regular dance practice into your routine. Allow yourself the freedom to explore both choreographed sequences and spontaneous expressions within your dance. Notice how each movement feels in your body—how it affects your mood, your energy levels, and your connection with yourself.

Belly dance invites you on a transformative journey. It encourages you to explore new realms of self-expression and healing, promising not just better physical health but a richer, more harmonious life experience. Embrace this beautiful art form; let it guide you toward deeper connections with yourself and the world around you as you continue on your path to personal fulfillment and well-being.

Starting a belly dance practice during recovery requires a gentle, mindful approach:

1. **Begin with subtle movements, gradually increasing intensity as strength and confidence grow:** Start with gentle, controlled motions that do not strain the body. As your physical condition improves, you can gradually incorporate more complex and dynamic movements, always listening to your body's signals.
2. **Work with an instructor to develop modifications that accommodate individual needs and limitations:** A knowledgeable instructor can tailor the dance to suit your recovery needs, offering variations of movements that protect vulnerable areas while still promoting engagement and progress.
3. **Focus on how movements feel internally rather than their external appearance:** Pay close attention to the sensations within your body as you move. This inward focus helps you connect deeply with your healing process, ensuring that each movement supports recovery rather than hinders it.
4. **Establish a comfortable, private environment for your initial dance practice:** Creating a space where you feel safe and at ease is crucial. This allows you to explore movement without self-consciousness or external pressure, fostering a positive and empowering practice environment.
5. **Consider incorporating props like veils or silk fans to aid movement and provide a sense of security:** Props can offer both physical support and emotional comfort, helping you to explore new movements with a sense of playfulness and security. They also add an element of artistry, allowing you to express yourself in ways that feel safe and rewarding.
6. **Practice mindfulness and patience throughout your journey:** Recovery is a process that requires both time and patience. By incorporating mindfulness techniques, such as deep breathing and meditation, you can maintain a positive mindset and stay connected to your goals. Celebrate small victories along the way

and remind yourself that progress, no matter how gradual, is still progress.
7. **Engage with a supportive community or group:** Connecting with others on a similar journey can provide encouragement, inspiration, and a sense of belonging. Whether online or in person, finding a community that understands your challenges and celebrates your achievements can make a significant difference in your recovery.

Emerging Trends in Dance and Wellness

The integration of dance into health care is a growing trend. More hospitals are developing specialized belly dance programs for various health conditions, recognizing its potential as a complementary therapy. The rise of online platforms is making dance therapy accessible to those unable to attend in-person classes, while emerging wearable technologies are allowing for more precise tracking of the dance's physical benefits.

Overcoming Barriers to Dance

Many individuals face barriers to starting dance, including concerns about age, fitness level, and body image. However, belly dance adapts to all ages and fitness levels. Instructors emphasize respectful approaches to practicing belly dance, honoring its cultural roots while making it accessible to a diverse group of participants.

The Transformative Power of Rhythm

Perhaps most profoundly, practitioners experience the transformative power of rhythm in their healing journey. Engaging with the varied rhythms of belly dance music can help regulate sleep-wake cycles, which are often disrupted by illness and stress. The complex rhythms enhance cognitive function and coordination, providing a mental workout alongside the dance's physical benefits.

As individuals continue their dance practice, many find that the rhythm becomes a metaphor for life itself—sometimes fast, sometimes slow, but always moving forward. In reclaiming life's rhythm through belly dance, practitioners not only recover physically but also discover a new depth of emotional resilience and spiritual connection.

The journey from struggle to empowerment through belly dance serves as a powerful testament to its healing potential. It reminds us that even in our darkest moments, there is a rhythm within, waiting to be awakened—a rhythm that can guide us back to wholeness, joy, and life itself.

References:

1. Koch, S. C., Riege, R. F. F., Tisborn, K., Biondo, J., Martin, L., & Beelmann, A. (2019). Effects of dance movement therapy and dance on health-related psychological outcomes. A meta-analysis update. *Frontiers in Psychology*, 10, 1806.
2. Rodrigues-Krause, J., Krause, M., & Reischak-Oliveira, A. (2019). Dancing for healthy aging: functional and metabolic perspectives. *Alternative Therapies in Health and Medicine*, 25(1), 44-63.
3. Fong Yan, A., Cobley, S., Chan, C., Pappas, E., Nicholson, L. L., Ward, R. E., ... & Hiller, C. E. (2021). The effectiveness of dance interventions on physical health outcomes compared to other forms of physical activity: a systematic review and meta-analysis. *Sports Medicine*, 51(4), 863-913.
4. McNeely, M. E., Duncan, R. P., & Earhart, G. M. (2015). A comparison of dance interventions in people with Parkinson disease and older adults. *Maturitas*, 81(1), 10-16.
5. Lazarou, I., Parastatidis, T., Tsolaki, A., Gkioka, M., Karakostas, A., Douka, S., & Tsolaki, M. (2017). International ballroom dancing against neurodegeneration: A randomized controlled trial in Greek community-dwelling elders with mild cognitive impairment. *American Journal of Alzheimer's Disease & Other Dementias*, 32(8), 489-499.
6. Bräuninger, I. (2012). Dance movement therapy group intervention in stress treatment: A randomized controlled trial (RCT). *The Arts in Psychotherapy*, 39(5), 443-450.
7. Moe, A. M. (2012). Beyond the belly: An appraisal of middle eastern dance (aka belly dance) as leisure. *Journal of Leisure Research*, 44(2), 201-233.

9

THE UNEXPECTED CALL TO CONNECT

The warm Gulf Coast sunlight filtered through the windows of my new home in Biloxi, Mississippi, illuminating my graceful movements as I danced. At fifty-four years young now, I found myself reflecting on the unexpected chapter of my life that began four years ago, far from the familiar streets of my French-Canadian hometown. Belly dance had long been the rhythm of my heart, a cherished companion that had guided me through life's twists and turns. For years, I had the joy of sharing this beautiful art form with others, watching as it transformed not just bodies but spirits too. Now, it acted as both a familiar comfort and a bridge to creating community in this new Southern coastal setting, proving its power in navigating life's unexpected changes.

My journey to Biloxi, a place I never imagined calling home, began on January 9, 2020, when I was fifty years young. My initial intention was simple: to learn ballroom dance from Percell St. Thomass at his dance school, DanceKinesis. I planned to study for two months, gaining skills I could bring back to teach at my grandson's French Catholic elementary school in Canada. However, as I soon discovered, the universe had different plans for me.

One February day, barely a month into my stay, as I drove back to my temporary residence after a dance lesson, I experienced what I could only describe as a message from my higher self. "This is your home now." The realization shook me to my core, but I knew with certainty that it was meant to be. This moment of clarity felt like an awakening of my crown chakra, connecting me to a higher purpose and universal wisdom.

With trembling hands, I called my husband back in Canada to share this revelation. His response left me breathless. He revealed that in 2018, during a sauna session, he had received a spiritual message that said, "Your wife will be going south." In that moment, his heart overflowed with unconditional love, and he understood that true love sometimes means setting the other person free. With a bittersweet mixture of devotion and sacrifice, he knew he would need to let me spread my wings, even if it meant watching me fly away. He chose not to share this insight with me. However, not knowing when this would happen, he continued to keep cherishing our beautiful relationship, with committing to making every day count, hoping that our time together would stretch on as long as possible. In the meantime, he quietly created art pieces of monarch butterflies as a personal reminder of my forthcoming transformation.

I was deeply touched and moved by his selfless love, yet simultaneously gripped by fear. How could I make this unfamiliar place my home if I was all alone? Despite these fears, I had no doubt that my higher self knew the path forward. This synchronicity felt like a powerful alignment of our heart chakras, demonstrating the deep connection and selfless love we shared, while also highlighting the profound trust I needed to place in my own inner guidance.

The decision to stay in Mississippi was the most difficult I had ever made. I was leaving behind not just my loving husband but also my only daughter, my grandson whom I saw almost daily, my mother, and my father. My daughter was really worried about me; she thought I was going through a midlife crisis. I didn't blame her for her concern—everything was happening so fast. But I reassured her that it was all divine timing. This calling was undeniable. It resonated deep within my solar plexus chakra, igniting a sense of personal power and purpose I couldn't ignore, even as I acknowledged the impact it was having on my loved ones.

Little did I know that my decision would be tested in ways I couldn't have imagined. On April 16, 2020, my father passed away. The pain of this loss was compounded by the fact that I couldn't return to Canada for his funeral due to the COVID-19 travel restrictions and my decision not to get vaccinated. This separation from my family during such a crucial time made my journey even more challenging, forcing me to find new ways to process my grief and honor my father's memory from afar.

As I continued my ballroom dance training, I found myself spending more time with Jamie, whom I had met through the local ballroom scene before COVID-19 hit. He had volunteered to be my dance partner, offering to practice with me regularly. Our connection was instant and profound, triggering memories of what felt like another lifetime—a soul I had loved and lost, now found again. This realization made my decision both clearer and more mystical, as if the universe was revealing its grand design. The energy between us felt like a perfect balance of masculine and feminine, each complementing and strengthening the other. As we danced together, our growing bond created an alchemical transformation, turning the lead of uncertainty into the gold of destiny, further affirming my decision to stay while infusing my journey with a sense of magical synchronicity.

This magical connection catalyzed a whirlwind of change in my life. With a mixture of emotion and practicality, I filed for divorce from my Canadian husband, Leo Levac, who, in his unconditional love, remained a cherished friend and my "warrior loving husband." The universe seemed to move at an accelerated pace, and on July 16, 2020, just one day after finalizing my divorce and a mere seven months after my arrival in Biloxi, I married Jamie Gilbert. As I embraced this new chapter of my life with open arms, I felt a powerful transformation sweeping through me. It was reminiscent of the fire element in belly dance—intense, passionate, and purifying—burning away the old and forging a new path forward with unwavering clarity and purpose.

As the world grappled with the onset of COVID-19, my ballroom dance aspirations were temporarily put on hold. In this pause, intensified by the grief of losing my father and the inability to be with my family, I found myself drawn back to my beloved belly dance. As I swayed to the rhythmic beats of Middle Eastern music in my new home, I realized that this ancient art form, with its universal appeal, could be my bridge to connecting with my new community and a powerful tool for healing.

The grounding movements of belly dance helped me feel rooted in my new home, connecting me to the earth element and strengthening my root chakra. The fluid hip circles and undulations reminded me of the water element, helping me adapt to the changes in my life with grace and flexibility. The fiery shimmies and sharp accents ignited my passion and transformation, while the graceful arm movements and turns connected me to the air element, giving me a sense of freedom and new possibilities.

As I continued to dance and teach over the past four years, I found that the principles of chakra alignment, the balance of feminine and masculine energies, and the embodiment of elemental forces that I had long taught in my belly dance classes were now guiding me through this major life transition. The practice became more than just a dance; it was a way of processing my emotions, connecting with my new environment, and rediscovering myself.

Alongside belly dance, I discovered that art, in its many forms, played a crucial role in my healing journey. Just as my cherished Leo had created butterfly art pieces as a symbol of my transformation, I found myself drawn to creative expression as a means of processing my experiences. Whether through painting, writing, or other artistic endeavors, I found that art provided a unique language for expressing emotions that were sometimes too complex for words alone. This creative process became another powerful tool for self-discovery and healing, complementing the transformative power of belly dance.

This journey of transformation was possible because I had truly aligned with my path. The uncertainty that initially clouded my decision became clear as I listened to my inner wisdom and followed the signs the universe was showing me. Through belly dance and artistic expression,

I was able to integrate all aspects of myself—physical, emotional, and spiritual—and find harmony in this new chapter of my life.

My story is a testament to the transformative power of belly dance and art and the importance of aligning with one's true path. When we open ourselves to the wisdom of our bodies, the balance of energies within us, and the elemental forces around us, we can navigate even the most unexpected turns in life with grace and purpose.

As I reflect on this journey at fifty-four, I am filled with gratitude for the way belly dance and art have supported me through this transition. They have been my constant companions, helping me to stay grounded while also embracing change. Through teaching, dancing, and creating, I have found my place in this new community and discovered new depths of self-understanding and personal growth.

This experience has deepened my belief in the holistic nature of artistic expression, whether through movement or visual arts. It is not just a form of exercise or creativity but a powerful tool for personal transformation, emotional healing, and spiritual growth. By embodying the principles of chakra alignment, energy balance, and elemental forces through dance and art, we can navigate life's challenges and embrace new beginnings.

As I continue to teach and create here on the Gulf Coast, I am excited to share these transformative aspects of belly dance and art with others. Whether they are facing major life changes, seeking to connect more deeply with themselves, or simply looking for a joyful way to express their inner worlds, I believe that dance and art have something profound to offer everyone.

My unexpected journey to Biloxi has shown me that when we truly align with our path, the uncertainty becomes clear. By staying open to the messages of our higher selves, honoring the wisdom of our bodies, and embracing the transformative power of artistic expression, we can find our way home—wherever that may be.

Life is the dancer and you are the dance.
—Eckhart Tolle

CULMINATING INSIGHTS: DEEPENING POWER AND CONNECTION THROUGH BELLY DANCE

This chapter reinforces that belly dance is much more than exercise or art. It is a powerful medium for self-expression, community building, and personal transformation. It helps participants create a new cultural identity while facilitating their adaptation to new environments. My journey highlights how belly dance not only supports physical health but also fosters an emotional release and a spiritual awakening through the balancing of chakras and the integration of elemental energies.

Belly dance continues to be a tool that helps me navigate the complexities of change and transition, offering a grounding and stabilizing force amid the upheaval of life's shifting circumstances. Through this dance, I have found a way to honor my years of experience while also embracing the new growth that comes with change, creating a sense of continuity and resilience in the face of uncertainty.

EMBRACING THE HOLISTIC IMPACT OF BELLY DANCE

As I continue to teach and practice belly dance on the Gulf Coast of Mississippi, I'm reminded of its profound holistic impact. I've witnessed how this art form nurtures not just the body but also the mind and spirit. It allows dancers, both novice and experienced, to express and process deep-seated emotions, promoting a release that is vital for overcoming life's challenges by rediscovering oneself.

In my classes, I guide students through movements that reflect strength and grace, helping them balance memories of home with the realities of their new lives—a journey I deeply understand. The practice aligns with the chakras, enhancing personal growth and emotional equilibrium, concepts I've explored and shared throughout my teaching career.

As we engage with the elemental energies of earth, water, fire, and air through our movements, I see my students tap into a primal source of power and vitality. This connection helps restore balance and harmony to their lives, just as it has done for me in this new chapter of mine.

By embodying these elemental qualities, we cultivate a deeper sense of connection to the natural world and to the fundamental forces that shape our existence.

INTEGRATING BELLY DANCE INTO LIFE FOR BALANCE AND FULFILLMENT

On the Gulf Coast of Mississippi, I've found that my regular engagement with belly dance continues to deepen my bodily connections, aligning my internal rhythms with external expressions, while fostering both physical and emotional balance. This integration reflects the ancient wisdom and spiritual rejuvenation I've always cherished about belly dance, in which it acts as a bridge between the physical and metaphysical realms.

By maintaining belly dance as a consistent part of my life, even after relocating, I've created a sacred space for self-care, self-discovery, and self-transformation. The practice becomes a refuge from the stresses and demands of daily life, a place where I can reconnect with my authentic self and find a renewed sense of purpose and meaning. This is a gift I strive to share with my new Gulf Coast community.

LEVERAGING BELLY DANCE FOR COMMUNITY CONNECTION AND PERSONAL GROWTH

The communal aspect of belly dance has taken on new significance for me in this coastal region. It extends beyond personal growth to offer a space for cultural exchange and mutual support. As I build a new dance community here, I'm enhancing my own feelings of belonging while easing the cultural transitions of others. This shared experience provides not just solace but also empowerment as we navigate our new lives with confidence fostered by a collective wisdom.

Through the connections forged in this new belly dance community, I've found a network of support and encouragement that helps me weather life's challenges while celebrating its joys. The bonds created through dance continue to be some of the most profound and enduring relationships in my life, offering a sense of kinship and understanding that transcends the boundaries of time and place.

CONCLUSION: A CONTINUING JOURNEY OF JOY AND SELF-DISCOVERY THROUGH BELLY DANCE

As I reflect on this unexpected turn in my life's journey, I reaffirm the transformative power of belly dance. More than the art form I've taught for years, it continues to be a holistic practice that integrates physical fitness, emotional release, and spiritual awakening, offering a path to a harmonious balance in life.

My story on the Gulf Coast of Mississippi is a testament to the ways in which belly dance can guide us through life's unexpected turns. What began as a short trip to learn ballroom dance has blossomed into a new chapter filled with purpose and community. Through belly dance, I've found a way to honor my past experiences while embracing the new opportunities that lie ahead.

As I continue to teach and grow in this new setting, I'm reminded that the journey of self-discovery through belly dance is never truly complete. Each class I lead, each performance I give, and each new connection I make adds another layer to this rich tapestry of experience. I look forward to the continued unfolding of this beautiful, unexpected path. I am grateful for the wisdom of belly dance that has guided me thus far and am excited for the new insights yet to come.

EPILOGUE

THE JOURNEY CONTINUES

As we come to the close of this transformative exploration, let us reflect on the profound impact that belly dance can have on every aspect of our lives. Throughout these pages, we have delved into the physical, emotional, and spiritual dimensions of this ancient art form, uncovering its potential to heal, empower, and inspire us in ways we may have never imagined.

We began by recognizing belly dance as more than just exercise or entertainment but as a gateway to personal transformation and holistic well-being. Through the alchemy of movement and music, we discovered how this dance can help us tap into our deepest emotions, release suppressed traumas, and cultivate a profound sense of self-awareness and acceptance.

As we explored the interplay of feminine and masculine energies within the dance, we gained a deeper understanding of how to balance these forces within ourselves, leading to greater harmony and resilience in all aspects of life. We learned to harness the power of the elements—earth, water, fire, and air—to ground us, cleanse us, ignite our passions, and set our spirits free.

The journey has also led us to confront and overcome the fears, misconceptions, and societal conditioning that can hold us back from fully embracing our authentic selves. Through the practice of belly dance, we discovered the courage to be vulnerable, to express our true emotions, and to celebrate our unique beauty and strength.

We've witnessed the transformative effects of belly dance in times of transition and change as a powerful tool for navigating life's shifting circumstances. Through various stories, we've seen how belly dance can serve as a lifeline to one's cultural roots and a bridge to new communities and experiences.

Perhaps most importantly, we've come to understand belly dance as a practice of self-love, self-care, and self-discovery. Each shimmy, each undulation, each graceful gesture became an opportunity to connect with our bodies, hearts, and souls in a deeper, more meaningful way. Through this journey, we have reclaimed our personal sovereignty by embracing our power to make choices that honor our authentic selves and our unique paths.

As we step forward into the world, let us carry this wisdom with us, remembering that the true eloquence of our dance lies not just in the precision of our technique but in the authenticity and depth of our expression. Let us approach each movement, each gesture, each breath with the same intention and presence that we bring to our lives as a whole.

May we continue to dance with passion and purpose, to embrace our vulnerabilities and our power, to honor our grief and our joy, and to celebrate the unbreakable spirit within us all. May we find in this ancient art a timeless source of healing, wisdom, and connection—to ourselves, to each other, and to the great web of life that unites us.

The journey of belly dance is a journey of the soul, and it is one that never truly ends. As we move forward, let us do so with grace, compassion, and an open heart, ready to embrace the rhythms of life in all their beauty and complexity.

Keep dancing, keep exploring, keep growing. Trust the wisdom of your body, the power of your emotions, and the resilience of your spirit. With each step, sway, and shimmy—with each breath—you reclaim your birthright to a life of wholeness, harmony, and joy.

The music plays on, the ancient rhythms pulse through our veins, calling us back to the eternal dance of life. May we answer that call with courage, with gratitude, and with an open heart, knowing that the journey itself is the destination and that the dance is always worth dancing.

As you continue on your path, remember that you are part of a global community of dancers, all exploring, growing, and shining their light. Know that the greatest gift you can give to yourself and to the world is the gift of your own authentic, radiant, and joyful presence.

May your dance be a prayer, a celebration, and a sacred offering to the beauty and mystery of life. And may it always lead you back home to the truth of who you are—a divine being of love, light, and infinite possibility.

With love and gratitude, your fellow dancer on the path of life,
Joany

ADDENDUM

Guide to Movements and Music for Elemental Energies, Feminine/Masculine Balance, and Chakra Activation

As we've explored the transformative power of belly dance through this book, we've touched on the profound connections between movement, energy, and personal growth. This addendum serves as a bonus section, offering a more in-depth look at how specific belly dance movements and musical choices can be used to cultivate balance and harmony within the body, mind, and spirit.

By working with the elemental energies of earth, water, fire, and air, we can tap into the primal forces that shape our physical, emotional, and spiritual experiences. Each element carries its own unique qualities and sensations, which can be expressed through targeted belly dance techniques and intentions.

Similarly, by consciously exploring and balancing the feminine and masculine energies within us, we can promote greater wholeness and authenticity in our dance practice and in our lives. The fluid, receptive flow of the feminine and the strong, dynamic drive of the masculine are both essential aspects of our being. By learning to express and integrate these energies, we can unlock new levels of personal power and creative potential.

Finally, working with the chakra system can be a powerful way to bring greater awareness, vitality, and balance to our body's energy centers. Each of the seven main chakras corresponds to specific physical, emotional, and spiritual qualities. By focusing on these energy centers through specific belly dance movements and musical choices, we can support their optimal functioning and promote our overall well-being.

This addendum provides a detailed guide to exploring the energetic dimensions of belly dance, with specific recommendations for movements and music that can enhance your practice and deepen your personal transformation.

FEMININE/MASCULINE ENERGY BALANCE

Feminine Energy

To cultivate and express the receptive, intuitive qualities of feminine energy, focus on graceful, flowing, and circular techniques.

Key Movements:

- Slow, sinuous undulations. Initiate from your chest, letting the movement ripple down.
- Fluid hip circles and figure eights. Trace soft, continuous patterns in space.
- Elegant, flowing arm gestures. Imagine gathering and releasing silk scarves in the air.
- Graceful, swaying steps. Move like a willow tree dancing in the wind.

Practice Tip: Spend time in nature observing recurring patterns and rhythms. Notice the changing seasons, lunar phases, or growth cycles of plants. This can help you connect with the ebb and flow of natural energies, which are associated with feminine energy in many traditions.

Music: Choose tracks with soft, melodic rhythms. Look for instruments like the oud, harp, or violin.

Recommended Songs:

1. "Sawah" by Dr. Samy Farag
2. "Ya Dale Ya Rohi" by Waell Kfoury
3. "Batwanes Beek" by Warda

Masculine Energy

To embody and express the strong, assertive qualities of masculine energy, focus on powerful, precise, and dynamic techniques.

Key Movements:

- Sharp, percussive hip accents. Imagine striking a drum with each movement.
- Strong, directional chest movements. Push your sternum forward and back with purpose.
- Bold, decisive arm movements. Imagine holding and skillfully using a sword or staff.
- Grounded, powerful turns. Turn as if surveying your kingdom.

Practice Tip: Engage in focused, goal-oriented activities to cultivate masculine energy.

Music: Select tracks with bold, energetic rhythms. Look for percussion instruments like the darbuka, riq, or daf.

Recommended Songs:

1. "Shimmabulous" by Issam Houshan
2. "Ela Rohi" by Oka Wi Ortega
3. "Sohab Awanta" by Hakim

CHAKRA ACTIVATION

Root Chakra (Muladhara)

Focus: Grounding, stability, and security

Key Movements:

- Slow, deep hip drops. Feel yourself sinking into the earth with each drop.
- Powerful, earthy undulations. Initiate from your pelvic floor, moving up through your spine.
- Strong, centered pelvic tilts and circles. Connect your physical body with the material world.
- Low, steady shimmies. Imagine sending roots deep into the ground.

Recommended Songs:

1. "Tabla Solo" by Hamid El Shari
2. "Masmoudi Sar'ye" by Issam Houshan
3. "Colors of Life" by Artem Uzunov

Sacral Chakra (Svadhisthana)

Focus: Creativity, sensuality, and emotional flow

Key Movements:

- Slow, flowing hip circles. As if stirring a large pot of creative energy.
- Graceful figure eights. Let the movement flow through your hips and torso.
- Fluid, sensual rib cage slides. Paint your desires in the air with your body.
- Playful, flirtatious hip accents and shimmies. Express your emotional freedom.

Recommended Songs:

1. "Yah Wahley" by Phil Thornton
2. "Helwa Ya Baladi" by Dalida
3. "Serpent's Rapture" by Mosavo

Solar Plexus Chakra (Manipura)

Focus: Personal power, confidence, and self-esteem

Key Movements:

- Sharp, percussive hip accents and drops. Ignite your inner fire.
- Powerful, expansive undulations. Radiate energy outward through your torso.
- Dynamic, outward-reaching arm movements. Express self-assurance.
- Fast, fiery shimmies. Channel the energy of transformation.

Recommended Songs:

1. "Amarin" by Amr Diab
2. "Chicky" by Oojami
3. "Ya Rayah" by Rachid Taha

Heart Chakra (Anahata)

Focus: Love, compassion, and emotional healing

Key Movements:

- Gentle, flowing arm movements. Reach out to embrace the world.
- Graceful, undulating chest circles and slides. Let love ripple outward.
- Soft, expansive turns. Open yourself up to giving and receiving love.
- Gentle hip sways. Rock with a comforting rhythm.

Recommended Songs:

1. "Hayart Albi Maak" by Mahmoud Fadl
2. "El Alam Elnai" by Magida El Roumi
3. "Ya Rait" by Ragheb Alama

Throat Chakra (Vishuddha)

Focus: Self-expression, communication, and authenticity

Key Movements:

- Gentle, flowing head slides and circles. Nod in agreement with your inner truth.
- Fluid, undulating arm movements and hand gestures. Express yourself clearly.
- Soft neck rolls. Release tension and blockages in your throat.
- Playful, improvisational hip and torso accents. Embrace your creative freedom.

Recommended Songs:

1. "I Love You" by Charbel Rouhana
2. "Shibbak Habibi" by Tony Mouzayek
3. "Sorna Soloh" by Wael Kfoury

Third Eye Chakra (Ajna)

Focus: Intuition, wisdom, and inner vision

Key Movements:

- Slow, meditative undulations. Trace the infinite wisdom of the universe.
- Gentle, inward-focused hip circles and slides. Spiral inward toward your center.

- Slow, deliberate turns. Turn your attention to your inner guidance.
- Subtle, mindful hand and arm gestures. Connect with your intuitive understanding.

Recommended Songs:

1. "Napas" by Mercan Dede
2. "Sufi" by Omar Faruk Tekbilek
3. "Shyam" by Deva Premal

Crown Chakra (Sahasrara)

Focus: Spiritual connection, enlightenment, and unity of consciousness

Key Movements:

- Gentle, upward-flowing undulations. Reach toward the heavens.
- Subtle, blissful head and upper body sways. Let energy cascade through your being.
- Light, effortless turns. Spin in a state of ecstatic oneness.
- Ethereal, expansive arm patterns. Surrender to divine grace.

Recommended Songs:

1. "Dream" by Marcel Khalife
2. "Seventh Heaven Suite" by Dhafer Youssef
3. "Waking State" by Anouar Brahem

FUTURE EXPLORATION: TWELVE CHAKRA BELLY DANCE

While we have focused on the seven primary chakras in this guide, the journey of energetic exploration through belly dance doesn't end here. I'm excited to announce that I am developing a future course that will delve deeper into the concept of twelve chakras and their expression through belly dance.

This course will expand on the foundation we've built, exploring five additional energy centers beyond the traditional seven. These include the following:

1. **Earth Star Chakra:** Grounding and connecting to the energy of the earth
2. **Soul Star Chakra:** Higher consciousness and spiritual evolution
3. **Transpersonal Point:** Universal connection and cosmic awareness
4. **Causal Chakra:** Manifestation and divine timing
5. **Stellar Gateway:** Connecting to the divine and universal wisdom

Through specific belly dance movements, music, and meditative practices, we'll explore how to activate and balance these extended energy centers. This course will offer a unique opportunity to deepen your spiritual practice, enhance your energetic awareness, and expand your belly dance repertoire.

The Twelve Chakra System allows for a more comprehensive understanding of our multidimensional nature, bridging the physical with the spiritual in profound ways. By incorporating these concepts into belly dance, we open new pathways for healing, growth, and transformation.

Stay tuned for more information about this exciting new course. It promises to be a transformative journey, taking your practice of belly dance as a spiritual art form to new heights.

ELEMENTAL ENERGIES

Earth

To embody the grounding, stabilizing energy of the earth element, focus on belly dance techniques that emphasize a deep connection to the ground and a sense of rootedness.

Key Movements:

- Wide, grounded stance. Feel the solid support of the earth beneath your feet.
- Powerful, slow hip drops. Imagine planting seeds with each movement.
- Deep, earthy undulations. Visualize roots growing from your feet, anchoring you to the ground.
- Strong, rooted shimmies. Shake off tension while allowing the earth's vitality to flow through you.

Practice Tip: Stand barefoot on natural ground when possible to enhance your connection to the earth element.

Music: Choose tracks with steady, pulsing beats. Look for percussion instruments like the doumbek, djembe, or frame drum.

Recommended Songs:

1. "Aziza" by Hossam Ramzy
2. "Desert Rose" by Sting featuring Cheb Mami
3. "Ya Bent El-Eih" by Tamer Hosny

Water

To tap into the fluid, graceful energy of the water element, focus on smooth, continuous, and flowing movements.

Key Movements:

- Fluid hip circles. Let the movement ripple through your torso and limbs like waves.
- Snakelike undulations. Imagine water coursing through your body, cleansing as it goes.
- Graceful figure-eight patterns. Paint infinity symbols with your hips and chest.
- Flowing arm movements. Let your arms spiral like ribbons of water.

Practice Tip: Observe bodies of water in nature, noticing their constant flow and adaptability.

Music: Select tracks with a soft, melodic flow. Look for instruments like the ney flute, oud, or violin.

Recommended Songs:

1. "Habibi Ya Nour El Ain" by Amr Diab
2. "Leilet Hob" by Umm Kulthum
3. "Tamally Maak" by Amr Diab

Fire

To embody the passionate, transformative energy of the fire element, focus on dynamic, energetic, and intense techniques.

Key Movements:

- Sharp, percussive hip accents. Imagine striking a match with each movement.
- Fast, shimmering shimmies. Let the vibrations travel through your entire body.
- Rapid, spinning turns. Envision yourself as a whirling dervish consumed by the intensity of fire.
- Bold, expressive arm gestures. Direct the fire's energy with your hands.

Practice Tip: Engage in regular activities that ignite your passion and creativity to connect with fire energy.

Music: Choose tracks with fast-paced, dynamic rhythms. Look for instruments like the mizmar, kanun, or darbuka.

Recommended Songs:

1. "Ya Tabtab Wa Dallaa" by Nancy Ajram

2. "Ya Habibi Taala" by Asmahan
3. "Awtar W'Haneen" by Hossam Ramzy

Air

To tap into the light, expansive energy of the air element, focus on graceful, fluid, and effortless movements.

Key Movements:

- Gentle, flowing arm patterns. Imagine conducting the wind with your hands.
- Soft, undulating torso circles. Let your ribcage expand and contract like a balloon.
- Graceful, spinning turns. Envision yourself as a leaf caught in a playful whirlwind.
- Light, buoyant hip movements. Move as if you were a feather riding the air currents.

Practice Tip: Incorporate deep breathing exercises to connect with the air element and gain new perspectives.

Music: Select tracks with light, airy melodies. Look for instruments like the ney, kawala, or wind chimes.

Recommended Songs:

1. "Whirling Dervish" by Omar Faruk Tekbilek
2. "Lamma Bada Yatathanna" by Al-Turath Ensemble
3. "A Dancer's Dream" by Raja Zahr

As you incorporate these movements and music into your belly dance practice, remember that this journey is uniquely yours. The goal isn't perfection but rather cultivating a deeper connection with yourself and the universal energies flowing through you. Trust your intuition and let your authentic expression shine through.

This guide is meant to serve as a resource and inspiration for your ongoing exploration of belly dance. Use it to enrich your practice, but don't be afraid to adapt and personalize these techniques to suit your individual needs and preferences.

Remember that belly dance is not just about mastering movements but about embracing a journey of self-discovery and transformation. Each practice session is an opportunity to deepen your understanding of yourself and the world around you.

As you continue to dance, may you find new depths of joy, healing, and connection. May each undulation, shimmy, and gesture bring you closer to your true essence and help you embody the beauty, strength, and wisdom that reside within you.

Embrace the transformative power of this ancient art form, and allow it to guide you toward greater self-awareness, inner peace, and holistic well-being. Your dance is a beautiful expression of your unique spirit—cherish it, nurture it, and share it with the world.

Keep dancing, keep exploring, and keep shining your light. The rhythm of life is calling—answer it with your whole being, one beautiful movement at a time.

With warmth and encouragement for your continued journey,
Joany

RESOURCES

Thank you for joining me on this transformative journey through *Feminicity: The Belly Dance Awakening*. To support your continued growth and exploration, here are additional resources, including those from some of the esteemed teachers I have studied with.

Online Resources and Community

While this book delves into the "why" of belly dance—its spiritual and transformative aspects—you can explore the practical "how" through the resources available at www.feminicity.net. This website serves as your comprehensive portal for all things related to belly dance and personal transformation. Here, you'll find the latest information on workshops and events, access to our supportive online community of like-minded individuals, and a wealth of practical resources including video tutorials, fitness routines, and virtual learning products. These online materials complement the book's teachings, allowing you to connect the inner journey explored in these pages with hands-on practice and community support. By combining the spiritual insights offered in this book with the practical guidance and connections available on the website, you can create a holistic belly dance experience that nurtures both your body and soul on this transformative path.

Local Belly Dance Communities

For the full experience and benefits described in this book, I highly recommend joining a local belly dance community. These in-person connections offer invaluable opportunities for growth, support, and shared learning. If you're on the Mississippi Gulf Coast, I teach classes locally and would be delighted to welcome you. For those in other areas, I encourage you to check your local community centers, dance studios, or online resources for belly dance classes near you. These gatherings provide a supportive environment to explore and deepen your practice alongside fellow dancers. Remember, the journey of belly dance is enriched by the connections we make and the community we build along the way. For the full experience and benefits described in this book, I highly recommend joining a local belly dance community. For more information about my classes or to connect with our belly dance community, please visit www.feminicity.net.

Further Reading

- *The Way of Belly Dancing* by Veena and Neena Bidasha
- *Grandmother's Secrets* by Rosina-Fawzia Al-Rawi
- *Serpent of the Nile* by Wendy Buonaventura

Online Belly Dance Resources

These are some of the teachers I have studied with:
Keti Sharif (A-Z Bellydance): ketisharif.com
Yasmina Ramzy Arts/Arabesque Academy: yasminaramzyarts.com
Shemiran Ibrahim: loveteachingbellydance.com
Alia Thabit: aliathabit.com
Jillina Carlano: jillina.com
Aziza of Montreal: aziza.tv
Khalida: khalidadance.com
Joana Saahirah: joanasaahirah.com
Dr. Kaouthar Darmoni: drkaouthardarmoni.com
Roula Said: roulasaid.com
Myra Krien (Pomegranate Studios): pomegranatestudio.org
Leslie Zehr: universaldancer.com

Connect with the Author

Follow me on social media:

- **Facebook:** Belly Dance on the Coast
- **Instagram:** Joany Gauvreau

YouTube Channels:

- @femonlinedance
- @feminicity

Remember, the journey of self-discovery through belly dance is deeply personal and unique to each individual. These resources are here to support and inspire you, but the most powerful tool you have is your own intuition and inner wisdom. Trust in your journey and keep dancing.